REAL PROSPERITY

GENE A. GETZ

MOODY PRESS

CHICAGO

ISBN: 0-8024-0892-3

2 3 4 5 6 7 8 Printing/VP/Year 95 94 93 92 91

Printed in the United States of America

This volume
is affectionately and sincerely dedicated
to my brothers and sisters in Christ
at Fellowship Bible Church North,
where I have the privilege of serving
as senior pastor.

Contents

Introduction

We are living in a materialistic world. Unfortunately, many of us are so affected by our present culture that we have lost focus on what the Bible says about material possessions. Interestingly God says more about how Christians are to view and use their material possessions than most any other subject, the chief exception being what God says about Himself. Such a realization emphasizes the importance of this subject.

A PERSONAL CHALLENGE

This book has evolved out of a unique experience in my life as a pastor. Challenged by a group of lay leaders in our church to do a series of messages on giving, I counterchallenged them to first of all join me in an extensive study of what the Bible has to say about material possessions. They enthusiastically agreed, and together we studied this subject throughout Scripture. We met for a number of months each Wednesday evening, discussing every reference to the subject in the entire Bible.

We tackled this task by way of *biblical theology.* We began with the founding of the church in the book of Acts and followed God's unfolding revelation throughout the New Testament, including Jesus' teachings in the gospels. At the same time, we looked at what God said about material possessions in the Old Testament, attempting to determine the continuity between the Old and New Covenants. Our research findings formed the biblical material for a series of messages I later delivered to the congregation.

A BIBLICAL THEOLOGY

These messages were eventually developed into an extensive work entitled *A Biblical Theology of Material Possessions* (also published by Moody Press). This volume follows in detailed and thorough fashion the flow of God's will as it is revealed chronologically throughout Scripture. The basic research design for this initial study, as well as the structure used in presenting these findings in written form, are illustrated in the graph on p. 11.

A SEQUEL

All of us—including my publisher—agreed that a second volume based on this material was needed. But the structure of this second book is quite different. It is based on a *systematic* and *thematic* approach. Whereas *A Biblical Theology of Material Possessions* outlines God's will as it unfolds throughout the New Testament era, *Real Prosperity* reflects the next step in doing theology—systematizing biblical truth. The 126 principles that emerged from the biblical theological study cluster around twelve basic themes in this second volume. These are found in chapters 1-13.

But the chronological unfolding of biblical history also determines the order in which these "clusters" appear. In fact, eight of these twelve themes (represented by chapter titles) emerge from God's dealings with the church in Jerusalem prior to its scattering. The rest of the themes come from God's work in the lives of His children as the church grew and expanded throughout the Roman world. What initially appears as a foundational and basic concept or theme in the book of Acts is often refined and expanded in the gospels and epistles as New Testament history progresses. Furthermore, just as each chapter grows out of God's unfolding revelation, the principles within each chapter also grow out of the same historical process.

INTEGRATING A BIBLICAL AND SYSTEMATIC APPROACH

The structure for this book, as well as the structure within each chapter, verifies why it is so helpful to first study biblical concepts as they appear sequentially in God's unfolding revelation. It enables us to move from doing *biblical theology* to a more *systematic approach* with the assurance that we are truly representing what God has unveiled for us over the process of time. This will become more meaningful as we proceed from concept to concept in the chapters to follow.

By referring to the Appendix, you will be able to see each principle in its historical and biblical context because these 126 principles are outlined and numbered chronologically. The Appendix has two features for each principle: a page reference and a symbol. The page number refers the reader to where the principle is discussed in the text. The symbol is designed to help communicate these concepts to others. I have used these symbols in presenting these principles in both seminar and sermon settings. They have proven to be a helpful technique in communicating these concepts.

As you read through *Real Prosperity*, you will also find references in the text to the Appendix. To help you integrate the systematic approach with the biblical approach used in *A Biblical Theology of Material Possessions*, a

A Historical and Chronological Structure for
Determining God's Will Regarding Material Possessions

PART I
THE CHURCH IN JERUSALEM

Acts 1:1–Acts 7:60

Supracultural Principles

PART II
THE TEACHINGS OF JESUS CHRIST

The Four Gospels

Matthew (60's A.D.)
Mark ('50's A.D.)
Luke (60 A.D.)
John (85-90 A.D.)

Supracultural Principles

PART III
MOVING BEYOND JERUSALEM

Acts 8:1–11:30

Supracultural Principles

PART IV
THE GENTILE CHURCH & ITS EXPANDED MISSION

Acts 13:1–15:35

James (45-50 A.D.)
Galatians (49-55 A.D.)

Supracultural Principles

PART V
PAUL'S MISSION

Acts 15:36–18:22

1 Thessalonians (51 A.D.)
2 Thessalonians (51 A.D.)
1 Corinthians (56 A.D.)
2 Corinthians (57 A.D.)

Supracultural Principles

PART VI
PAUL'S MISSION CONTINUED & HIS ROMAN IMPRISONMENT

Acts 18:23–28:31

Romans (58 A.D.)
Philemon (61 A.D.)
Ephesians (61 A.D.)
Colossians (61 A.D.)
Philippians (61 A.D.)

Supracultural Principles

PART VII
FINAL YEARS OF THE NEW TESTAMENT ERA

Beyond the Book of Acts

1 Timothy (63 A.D.), Titus (65 A.D.)
2 Timothy (66 A.D.), 1 Peter (63 A.D.)
Hebrews (64-68 A.D.), Jude (70-80 A.D.)
2 Peter (66 A.D.), 1,2,3 John (90 A.D.)
Revelation (90's A.D.)

Supracultural Principles

PART VIII
APPLYING BIBLICAL PRINCIPLES

Practical methodology applying supracultural principles in our church, our families and our personal lives code appears each time a principle is stated. For instance, if "SCP 23" occurs in parentheses, it refers to supracultural principle 23 in the Appendix. Turning to the Appendix will allow you to see the biblical context of this principle.

UTILIZING THIS MATERIAL

Hopefully the principles unfolded in this book will be as meaningful and life changing for you as they have been for me and for many of the people I serve as pastor. This thematic and systematic approach provides a practical way to study everything God has taught us regarding material possessions. To make it particularly helpful in a personal or group setting, a special evaluation and application exercise is included at the end of each chapter.

Today we hear a lot about material prosperity. In Christian circles the term "prosperity theology" has emerged. What is the correct perspective on the subject? *Real Prosperity* answers this question with a totally biblical and theological inquiry.

1

Penetrating a Materialistic World

One of the most obvious facts that stands out in the biblical record is that, as Christians, we are to impact non-Christians with our life-style, both personally and corporately. That kind of witness includes many things—our ethics, our morality, and our attitudes and actions toward others. However, no aspect of our life-style is illustrated more specifically and graphically in the New Testament than the way we view and use our material possessions. This aspect of our life-style stands out immediately in the New Testament as an important dynamic in penetrating the materialistic world with the gospel of Jesus Christ.

1. Encouraging Faith in Christ

There is a distinct correlation between how Christians use their material possessions and the way people respond to the message of salvation. This should not surprise us. God's great purpose in sending His Son into the world was to redeem sinful people. "I have come," Jesus proclaimed, "that they might have life and have it to the full" (John 10:10). Consequently, all that we have in this world in terms of material possessions can and should be used to achieve this purpose and to carry out the Great Commission of our Lord Jesus Christ (Matt. 28:19-20).

I am not speaking at this juncture of financially supporting missionaries and other Christian workers to enable them to carry out the Great Commission—though this should certainly be a prominent part of every Christian's life and experience. Money and ministry always go together. However, at this moment, I am referring to the way Christians use their material possessions as a means to demonstrate their deep love for one another.

THE CHURCH IS BORN

This principle is illustrated immediately and dramatically by the Christians in Jerusalem. God-fearing Jews had come from all over the New Testament world to participate in the Feast of Pentecost—a fifty-day celebration. On the final day—the Day of Pentecost—the Holy Spirit came and the church was born. Thousands of Grecian Jews who were converted to Jesus Christ decided to stay in Jerusalem rather than return to their homes in various parts of the Roman world.

This is understandable since they were unaware of God's timetable regarding the return of Christ. The revelatory fact that they were to be witnesses to the ends of the earth (Acts 1:8) became clouded in the midst of what was happening in their lives. They focused on one clear prophetic reality: Jesus Christ would return to Jerusalem as the reigning King. These God-fearing Jews were well aware of Zechariah's words: "On that day," he prophesied, "living water will flow out of *Jerusalem*. . . . The Lord will be king over the whole earth" (Zechariah 14:8-9).*

JESUS' NEW COMMANDMENT

Thousands of these new believers decided to stay in Jerusalem, no doubt waiting for the Messiah to return as He said He would. In the meantime, they began to practice in an extraordinary way the new commandment Jesus had given His disciples shortly before He went to the cross: "As I have loved you, so you must love one another." Jesus added, "All men will know that you are my disciples if you love one another" (John 13:34-35).

The Christians in Jerusalem immediately began to practice what Jesus had taught them. "Selling their possessions and goods, they gave to anyone as he had need" (Acts 2:45). Those who owned homes in Jerusalem opened their doors to those from other places in the world, and "they broke bread . . . and ate together with glad and sincere hearts." Through this great demonstration of love and unselfishness, these new believers began to penetrate the materialistic culture that characterized Judaism.[1] Luke recorded that they "were enjoying the favor of all the people." More and more Jews recognized that Jesus Christ was the true Messiah, "and the Lord added to their number daily those who were being saved" (Acts 2:47).

Though social and cultural dynamics vary today in different parts of the world, materialistic attitudes and actions have always been a part of people's lives worldwide, and it is still God's will that Christians use their possessions in ways that flesh out Christ's commandment to "love one another" in unselfish and nonmaterialistic ways. *When they do, those who do*

---

* In future Scripture quotations, all italics have been added for the sake of emphasis and will not be noted.

not know Jesus Christ personally will be encouraged to put their faith in Him (SCP 1)*.

2. HELPING THOSE WHO MAY RESENT US

Several years before the church was born, Jesus shared another startling commandment with His followers on a mountainside in Galilee. He exhorted them: "Give to the one who asks you, and do not turn away from the one who wants to borrow from you" (Matthew 5:42).

Jesus was dealing with basic attitudes toward those He identified as our *enemies*—those who may even hate us. Christ was teaching that we are not to demand "eye for eye" and "tooth for tooth" (Matthew 5:38). William Hendriksen summarizes this passage, concluding that "we have no right to hate the person who tries to deprive us of our possessions. Love even towards him should fill our hearts and reveal itself in our actions."[2]

Jesus was certainly not teaching that we should allow people to manipulate or take undue advantage of us. If we do, we are contributing to their irresponsibility. However, He was teaching that it is possible to use our material possessions to express, at least in a token way, the same love Christ demonstrated for His enemies when He gave His life for those who condemned Him and nailed Him to the cross.

When Stephen was being stoned because of his witness for Christ, "he fell on his knees and cried out, 'Lord, do not hold this sin against them'" (Acts 7:60). In essence, this is exactly what Christ did when He died on the cross. Looking down on His enemies, He cried, "Father, forgive them, for they do not know what they are doing" (Luke 23:34).

We can conclude that a Christian like Stephen, who demonstrated love toward those who were stoning him, would never hesitate to help meet the economic needs of his enemies (Matthew 5:42). Stephen has given us a remarkable demonstration of turning the other cheek (Matthew 5:39), of giving your "cloak as well as your tunic" (Matthew 5:40), and of going two miles when your enemy "forces you to go one mile" (Matthew 5:41).

Following the Day of Pentecost, Jerusalem was filled with Christians who were willing to practice these attitudes and actions toward their enemies—a marvelous demonstration of God's grace that enabled these believers to follow the teachings of Jesus Christ. In so doing, thousands of Jews responded to the gospel. *There is no greater demonstration of God's love in Christ than to take what belongs to us and share it with someone else— especially if that person is an enemy of the cross of Christ* (SCP 23).

Strange as it may seem, there are many opportunities in the world to practice this principle. All we need do is look for them. In our own church,

---

* Throughout this book, the letters *SCP* refer to a numbered *supracultural principle* found in the Appendix, which lists 126 principles concerning material possessions in a biblical and historical arrangement.

we have been intensely involved in supporting an inner-city ministry, not only with our material possessions but with our presence in that community. We began this process by financially supporting a mature Christian couple who lived in the area. The couple, in turn, created a setting and structure for our own people to minister in that culture. This involved, first of all, helping to purchase and refurbish a large facility to serve as a center to meet the material and emotional needs of people—including food, clothes, medical attention, and education. The meeting of such needs eventually led to the founding of a church in that culture.

3. VERIFYING GOD'S TRUTH

The Jerusalem believers demonstrated dramatically that *Christians who are unselfish and benevolent become a unique verification to non-Christians that Jesus Christ is indeed the Son of God* (SCP 49). The way they lived out their faith impacted the non-Christian world and encouraged people to respond in faith.

Several years later, a woman named Dorcas illustrated in a personal way this dynamic process of evangelism. Her love and good deeds were known throughout the city of Joppa (Acts 9:36). She used the skills she had, as well as her resources, to make clothes for needy people (Acts 9:39). Though it was the miracle of her resurrection at the hand of Peter that became a specific verification of the death and resurrection of Christ, it was also the beautiful example of her unselfish life-style that helped open the door for the gospel and added an enduring impact to Peter's miracle.

The world is and always has been filled with selfish people. Because of the principle of sin that is operative in all of us, we naturally tend to look out for ourselves. As a result, Christians such as Dorcas, who really care about others, stand out and form a unique verification that Jesus Christ is truly the Son of God, the one who can bring people who are dead in their "transgressions and sins" back to life (Ephesians 2:1).

4. PRACTICING A BIBLICAL WORK ETHIC

The Bible is exceedingly practical. Through His apostolic representatives, God has spoken to almost every situation in life. Interestingly, the diligence with which we Christians apply ourselves in the work-a-day world is an important factor in impacting non-Christians with the gospel.

Writing to the Thessalonians, Paul had to deal with the problem of laziness: "Make it your ambition to lead a quiet life, to mind your own business and to work with your hands, just as we told you so that your daily life may *win the respect of outsiders* and so that you will not be dependent upon anybody" (1 Thessalonians 4:11-12).

Perhaps these believers had heard about the Jerusalem Christians and how they cared for each other. Perhaps in their own poverty they had received gifts from benevolent Christians and had used this as an opportunity to take advantage of others' unselfishness. Or perhaps they were just so excited about the prospect of being delivered from their earthly circumstances that they were spending all of their time talking about the second coming of Christ and not working to earn a living. Whatever the circumstances, Paul had to admonish some of them.

The principle that God wants all Christians to learn and to apply is crystal clear in this New Testament letter. *Christians should work hard to provide for their economic needs so that they are not criticized by unbelievers for being lazy and irresponsible* (SCP 64).

Paul modeled this principle in his own personal ministry. Even though he had a right to financial support as a minister of the gospel (1 Corinthians 9:12), he did not use this right when he initially preached the gospel among the Thessalonians. "Surely you remember, brothers," he wrote, "our toil and hardship; we worked *night* and *day* in order not to be a burden to anyone while we preached the gospel of God to you" (1 Thessalonians 2:9).

As we will see in a future chapter, Paul was not teaching that Christian leaders should always preach the gospel without financial support. There are times when financial support is best and necessary. But the point is that the apostle Paul not only taught a strong work ethic, he also practiced it in his own life—even if it meant working "night and day." And most important, his motivation to work hard in this instance was to be a strong witness to people who did not know Christ as personal Savior.

5. Breaking Fellowship with Lazy Christians

Paul believed so strongly in practicing a biblical work ethic before the unsaved world that he actually exhorted Christians to *separate themselves from other believers who are persistently irresponsible* (SCP 65). When some of the Thessalonian Christians did not respond to his exhortations in his first letter, he zeroed in on the subject again in his second letter: "In the name of our Lord Jesus Christ, we command you, brothers, to *keep away from every brother who is idle* and does not live according to the teaching you received from us" (2 Thessalonians 3:6).

Initially, Paul exhorted them regarding this matter after he and his fellow missionaries led them to Christ (2 Thessalonians 3:10). When he later wrote to them, he reminded them of his own example as a missionary (1 Thessalonians 2:7-9). He also repeated in writing the exhortation to work hard to meet their own needs, something he had told them face-to-face (1 Thessalonians 4:11). Finally, he ended his first letter by asking all the Christians in Thessalonica to "warn those who are idle" (1 Thessalonians 5:14).

Against this backdrop, Paul's instructions regarding church discipline are understandable. Some of these believers had persistently and blatantly ignored both his example and his exhortations. It was time to take action.

This principle demonstrates dramatically how displeased God is when Christians do not work hard to earn a living and, in the process, take advantage of others. In a sense, Paul grouped "lazy Christians" into the same category as "immoral Christians" (1 Corinthians 5:1-2). Paul was underscoring that these sins bring reproach on the cause of Christ and cause people to reject the gospel.

Though this kind of discipline should be administered with a great deal of sensitivity and humility, it must be done if we intend to obey God. Since some of the Thessalonian Christians had been repeatedly taught what was proper and right regarding work habits, and since they refused to respond, they were to be excluded from the fellowship of believers.

This exhortation, of course, does not apply to believers who want to work but cannot. Rather, it applies to those who can work but will not. Hopefully, when this principle is applied in love, those involved will respond and walk in the will of God. This process in itself becomes an unusual witness to the watching world.[3]

6. Serving Employers with Diligence and Right Motives

Paul had some things to say that were even more specific regarding a Christian's work ethic: "Whatever you do, *work at it with all your heart*, as working for the Lord, not for men, since you know that you will receive an inheritance from the Lord as a reward. *It is the Lord Christ you are serving*" (Colossians 3:23-24).

The context for this exhortation related to slaves and the way they were to do their work. Though Paul did not condone slavery, he attacked this social disease by teaching slaves that the fastest way to freedom was to serve their masters as if they were serving God. They should obey not only when they were being watched (to "win their favor") but to obey with sincerity of heart and reverence for the Lord (Colossians 3:22). Paul was reminding these slaves that, in reality, they were serving the Lord Christ when they served their earthly masters (Colossians 3:24).

Translated into our culture today, the principle is clear. As Christian employees, *we should work hard to serve our employers* (whether Christian or non-Christian). And we are to do this *as if we are actually serving the Lord Jesus Christ* (SCP 104). In so doing, we become witnesses in this world. How tragic when Christians who are irresponsible in their work habits attempt to share the gospel with their employers and fellow employees. They bring reproach on Jesus Christ, as well as on His Body, the church.

7. Treating Employees Fairly and with Dignity

Paul quickly reminded the Colossians that what he was sharing with slaves was a two-way street. "Masters," he wrote, "provide your slaves with what is right and fair, because you know that you also have a Master in heaven" (Colossians 4:1). When Christians in the New Testament began to love their slaves as Christ loved them, it literally destroyed this social structure among believers.

Again, the principle is clear. Whereas Christian employees should work hard to serve their employers as if they were actually serving the Lord, conversely, *Christian employers should always treat their employees fairly—just the way they want God to treat them* (SCP 105).

Again, this fairness should be equally applied to Christians and non-Christians. There is no room for prejudice. Those who are in the role of employer should do everything they possibly can to encourage their employees. This involves paying them a living wage. And when employees work hard and faithfully to increase profits, the Christian employer should do everything he can to share those profits equitably with those who made it possible.

What a tremendous witness this would be to unsaved employees. Nothing would do more to establish trust, respect, and credibility. In this sense, "money talks!" Christian employers who treat their employees fairly and generously will have a listening ear when opportunities come to present the gospel of Jesus Christ.

NOTES

1. For an in-depth study of the materialism that permeated the Jewish life-style at this period in history, see Joachim Jeremias, *Jerusalem in the Time of Jesus*, trans. F. H. and C. H. Kay (London: SCM, 1969).

2. William Hendriksen, *New Testament Commentary: Exposition of the Gospel According to Matthew* (Grand Rapids: Baker, 1973), p. 310.

3. For a more extensive development of this sensitive subject, see Gene A. Getz, *A Biblical Theology of Material Possessions* (Chicago: Moody, 1990).

LET'S CHECK OURSELVES

On a scale of one to ten, circle the number that best represents how well you believe the people in your church or group practice the biblical principle found in each question.

1. Are people in our community coming to know Jesus Christ because they see the believers in our church demonstrating unselfish and generous use of their material possessions to further the kingdom of God?

VERY LITTLE				SOMEWHAT				EXTENSIVELY	
1	2	3	4	5	6	7	8	9	10

2. Do the people in our church actually reach out and help in material ways people who may actually resent them or the message of Jesus Christ?

VERY LITTLE   SOMEWHAT   EXTENSIVELY

1   2   3   4   5   6   7   8   9   10

3. Are the acts of benevolence and love by the people in our church impacting the non-Christian community with the message of the gospel?

VERY LITTLE   SOMEWHAT   EXTENSIVELY

1   2   3   4   5   6   7   8   9   10

4. Do people in our church maintain a strong work ethic so as to be a good example to those in the community who do not know Christ?

VERY LITTLE   SOMEWHAT   EXTENSIVELY

1   2   3   4   5   6   7   8   9   10

5. Do the leaders in our church apply principles of church discipline, in this case, as it relates to Christians who are lazy and irresponsible?

VERY LITTLE   SOMEWHAT   EXTENSIVELY

1   2   3   4   5   6   7   8   9   10

6. Do the people in our church perform their vocational tasks as if they were actually serving Jesus Christ?

VERY LITTLE   SOMEWHAT   EXTENSIVELY

1   2   3   4   5   6   7   8   9   10

7. Do the Christian employers in our church treat their employees in the same way they would like God to treat them?

VERY LITTLE   SOMEWHAT   EXTENSIVELY

1   2   3   4   5   6   7   8   9   10

How to Use This Evaluation Exercise

1. Duplicate these seven questions on a separate sheet, and have each person in your group anonymously evaluate your church.
2. Tabulate the responses to find an average score. To do so, total the numbers circled in each question. Divide this total number by the number of people responding to that particular question. This will give you a "mean," or average, score.
3. Discover the greatest needs in your church by arranging the scores numerically from the highest to the lowest. Those scores that are lowest represent the areas that need immediate attention.

4. In discussing these scores and the principles involved, spend time first of all reviewing the areas of strength in your church. Spend time in prayer, thanking God for those strengths.
5. Finally, spend time discussing ways to practice the principles that are the most neglected in your church. The following questions will help:
   a. What are the areas of greatest need?
   b. What can we do that we are not doing to practice these biblical principles?
   c. What specific goals can we set up to practice these principles?
   d. What can we do *immediately*?

PERSONALIZING THIS PROJECT

Once you've worked through this project at a group level, encourage each person to *individualize* this exercise by substituting personal pronouns (e.g., I, me, my). Thus, the first question would read, "Are people in our community coming to know Jesus Christ because they see *me* demonstrating unselfish and generous use of *my* material possessions to further the kingdom of God?" Then encourage each person to compare his or her scores with the averages of the group scores.

If you are working through this material on your own, you can immediately personalize these questions to determine how you measure up to God's standards.

2
Reaching Affluent People for Christ

Jesus came to die for the *whole* world—including people who have abundant material possessions. How can we reach these people with the gospel? To consider such a question so early in this book may seem unusual. In fact, it may threaten those of us who do not consider ourselves affluent. It may raise certain predictable questions in our own minds: Why emphasize reaching with the gospel people who have a lot of material possessions? Is this not a violation of the principle of equality when it comes to our human condition and needs? Furthermore, did not Jesus say it was difficult for wealthy people to respond to the gospel? Two reasons compel us to look at this subject early on.

The first is biblical. The book of Acts records that several prominent and wealthy people responded to the gospel immediately after the church was scattered out of Jerusalem because of persecution. In this sense, God Himself has modeled this approach for us by making it a priority in His evangelistic strategy. To be true to Scripture, we cannot ignore that.

The second reason for this sequence is pragmatic. People of means can help carry out the Great Commission in unusual ways. They are people who can witness to other people in prominent social positions, and they are people who can provide unusual amounts of money to help others preach the gospel. Furthermore, they can reach peers who have the potential to do the same.

Is this why we see affluent people coming to Christ in Luke's historical account immediately after the church was scattered? If we believe the Holy Spirit inspired Luke to record the events in the book of Acts, we must conclude that this is an important emphasis in God's evangelistic plan. In this sense, a biblical theology is also pragmatic. We must not separate the two.

1. Feeling No Need for God

In attempting to reach those who are wealthy, we must recognize that having a lot of material things does make it difficult for unsaved people to recognize and acknowledge their need of God. That is a major point Jesus was making to His disciples following His encounter with the rich young ruler. This man came to Jesus asking what "good thing" he must do to inherit eternal life (Matthew 19:16). To his surprise, Jesus told him to sell what he had and give the proceeds to the poor. Then he would "have treasure in heaven" (Matthew 19:21). But "when the young man heard this, he went away sad, because he had great wealth" (Matthew 19:22).

As the rich young ruler turned and walked away with sadness, Jesus told those who were watching and listening that it is "hard for a rich man to enter the kingdom of heaven." His disciples "were greatly astonished and asked, 'Who then can be saved?'" Jesus' response left the door wide open to every person—rich or poor: "With man this is impossible, but with God all things are possible" (Matthew 19:23-26).

SALVATION BY FAITH, NOT WORKS

It should be noted that Jesus was not teaching this young man or those listening that they must sell everything and give away the proceeds to be saved. This would contradict the whole of Scripture—for no one can be saved by doing good works (Romans 4:1-3; 5:1; Ephesians 2:8-9). Salvation is a gift from God that is received by faith.

What, then, was Jesus teaching? First, note that He did not require this kind of sacrifice from other rich people who followed Him. In the case of the rich young ruler, He was dealing with a man who was in love with his material possessions. He had "great wealth," and it was his stumbling block. Though he did a lot of good things with his life, his love of money kept him from experiencing God's saving love and grace. Evidently, he was not even willing to discuss the matter further with Jesus. He simply walked away with a heavy heart.

"BLESSED ARE THE POOR IN SPIRIT"

Jesus dealt with this subject in His Sermon on the Mount: "Blessed are the poor in spirit, for theirs is the kingdom of heaven" (Matthew 5:3). With this statement, He was telling those who were poor, both materially and spiritually, to be encouraged. Though they had little of this world's goods, this could serve as a means to open their hearts to God. The fact that they were "poor in a material sense" enabled them to be "poor in spirit." To be rich may have given them a feeling of being "rich in spirit," which tends to interfere with a person's response to God's invitation to be saved. Unfortunately, people like the rich young ruler often feel no need for God when they feel "rich" and self-satisfied inside.

It is true, then, that *having a lot of material things often makes it difficult for people to recognize and acknowledge their need for God* (SCP 21). However, this principle does not mean that well-to-do people cannot or will not respond to the gospel. Zacchaeus (Luke 19) certainly illustrates that they do, and as we continue our study, we will encounter other prominent and well-to-do people who came to Christ. What can we learn from these biblical examples that will help us to reach affluent people with the gospel today?

2. Learning to Penetrate Culture

When attempting to reach people of means, we can learn a valuable principle of communication from Jesus. Since material needs, worldly possessions, and making a living are important to all people, we can utilize these concerns and needs as Jesus did in teaching spiritual truth. This was the rationale for the content in more than 25 percent of His parables. It is clear that our Lord Himself was attempting to communicate with well-to-do people. To be more specific, eleven out of thirty-nine of Jesus' parables deal directly with finances and money. Notice how and why He used these parables:

- Jesus referred to *investment* in jewels and treasures to illustrate the importance of investing in the kingdom of God (Matthew 13:44-45).
- He referred to *saving* new treasures, as well as old, to illustrate the importance of storing up both old and new truth (Matthew 13:52).
- He used *indebtedness* to illustrate the importance of forgiveness (the parable of the unmerciful servant—Matthew 18:23-35).
- He referred to *hiring* procedures and *wage* structures to illustrate God's sovereignty and generosity in treating all with equality, especially when forgiving sins and rewarding people with eternal life (the parable of the workers in the vineyard—Matthew 20:1-16).
- He told a story about a fruit farmer who *leased* his property to tenants to illustrate the way the chief priests and Pharisees were rejecting God and His Son (the parable of the tenants—Matthew 21:33-46; Mark 12:1-12; Luke 20:9-19).
- He discussed *capital, investments, banking,* and *interest* to emphasize our human responsibility to utilize God's gifts in a prudent and responsible way (the parable of the talents—Matthew 25:14-30; the parable of the ten minas—Luke 19:11-27).
- He referred to *money lenders, interest,* and *debt* cancellation to illustrate the importance of love and appreciation to God for canceling our debt of sin (Luke 7:41-43).

- He referred to *building barns to store grain* for the future while neglecting to store up spiritual treasures as a very foolish decision (the parable of the rich fool—Luke 12:16-21).
- He used *architectural planning*, *building construction*, and *cost analysis* to illustrate the importance of future planning and counting the cost before we make decisions in building our spiritual lives (Luke 14:28-30).
- He used the human joy that comes from finding *money* we have lost to illustrate the joy in the presence of angels when a lost soul believes in Christ (Luke 15:8-10).
- He used *wealth*, dividing up an *estate*, irresponsible *spending*, and a change of heart to illustrate repentance and forgiveness (the parable of the prodigal son—Luke 15:11-32).
- He used bad *financial management* and dishonest *debt reduction* to illustrate that dishonest business people are sometimes wiser in their worldly realm than honest followers of Christ in the spiritual realm (the parable of the shrewd manager—Luke 16:1-12).
- He contrasted a *rich man* who died and went to hell with a *poor beggar* who died and went to heaven to illustrate how wealth and what it provides can harden our hearts against spiritual truth (the parable of the rich man and Lazarus—Luke 16:19-31).
- He contrasted the proud Pharisee who fasted and *tithed* regularly with the humble tax collector who acknowledged his sin of *dishonesty* and *greed* to illustrate that God acknowledges humility and rejects self-exaltation (the parable of the Pharisee and the tax collector—Luke 18:9-14).
- He used a grain-ripened field and *harvesters* to illustrate the spiritually ripened hearts in Samaria and the part the apostles would have in harvesting people's souls (John 4:34-38).

JESUS' PURPOSE WITH THESE PARABLES

When Jesus told these parables, His purpose was not to evaluate various aspects of the economic policies and procedures used in Palestine. Rather, He was using what was most familiar in order to teach spiritual truth. He was tapping into what was uppermost in people's minds at all economic levels in an effort to capture their attention. He was penetrating their culture.

Today, as we communicate God's truth and teach people spiritual truths, *we should develop an awareness of the economic structures, practices, and experiences in every culture* (SCP 37). If the people we are trying to reach are going to respect us and listen to our message, we must—like Jesus—not only understand their particular world but also be able to touch their world with biblical truth.

We must also be able to do this with realistic applications that are true to the principles of Scripture. Here again we can learn another valuable lesson from Jesus. He touched the economic world in which He lived without compromise but also without attacking the economic structures that formed the bulwark of His particular society.

3. UNDERSTANDING GOD'S GRACE TOWARD UNINFORMED PEOPLE

When the church in Jerusalem was eventually scattered because of persecution, we are given some specific illustrations in the book of Acts of rich people who were touched with the gospel of Christ. As with all biblical examples, we can learn some valuable lessons. One of these lessons is that God is sometimes more patient with uninformed people who are materialistic than He is with people who have more direct exposure to the truth.

GOD'S GRACE TOWARD SIMON THE SORCERER

This principle is dramatically illustrated in the life of Simon the sorcerer. Simon was an affluent pagan who was using his prominent position in the Samaritan culture as a platform to lead many people astray. When Philip began to preach the gospel in Samaria, a number of Simon's followers shifted their allegiance to Jesus Christ. Intrigued and amazed by the miracles Philip was performing, Simon, too, professed belief in Christ and was baptized (Acts 8:13).

When the apostles in Jerusalem heard that the people in Samaria had responded to the Word of God, they sent Peter and John to assist Philip. The apostles prayed for these new Christians, and when they "placed their hands on them," the Samaritan believers experienced what had happened on the Day of Pentecost approximately five years earlier (Acts 8:15-17). We are not told specifically what transpired when the Spirit came on these new believers, but evidently there were—as at Pentecost—some unusual manifestations of spiritual power.

Watching these things happen triggered the sorcerer's vain imagination. He wanted the same power as the apostles. Operating from purely selfish motives, he offered Peter and John money for this supernatural ability (Acts 8:19). Peter's response was straightforward and uncompromising: "May your *money* perish with you, because you thought you could *buy the gift of God with money*" (Acts 8:20).

Simon wanted to "cash in" on a good thing. If he could have this kind of power, it would give him more wealth and an even greater position of prominence beyond anything he had ever experienced.

Years earlier, Peter had dealt with a couple in Jerusalem named Ananias and Sapphira. Following Barnabas's example of selling a piece of property and giving the proceeds to the apostles to distribute to needy Christians

(Acts 4:36-37), they "also sold a piece of property" in order to give money for the same purpose. However, Ananias and Sapphira had agreed together to keep back part of the money they received from the sale and to bring the remainder to the apostles while giving the impression that they were bringing it all.

The results were devastating. Both Ananias and Sapphira were much more severely judged for their deceitful behavior than was Simon. They literally lost their lives (Acts 5:1-11).

One difference between the way God dealt with this couple and the way He dealt with Simon seems to relate to their knowledge of God. Ananias and Sapphira knew Jesus Christ. They had probably heard Him teach. They certainly had heard a great deal of truth from the apostles' teachings.

Simon's experience was most different. Though he had professed faith, it appears that he did not have a true conversion experience. His knowledge of God was limited. Consequently, Peter expressed great concern for this man's spiritual welfare. He exhorted Simon to "repent of this wickedness and pray to the Lord." If he did, Peter told him that perhaps God would forgive him for having "such a thought" in his heart (Acts 8:21-22).

Comparing these two situations illustrates that *God is sometimes more patient with uninformed people who are materialistic than He is with people who have more direct exposure to the truth* (SCP 44). The more we know about God's will, the more accountable we are to live up to the light we have.

GOD'S GRACE TOWARD THE NINEVITES

This principle is verified in other situations in Scripture. For example, when God sent Jonah to preach to the pagan Ninevites, they responded in repentance. And, "when God saw what they did and how they turned from their evil ways, He had compassion and did not bring upon them the destruction He had threatened" (Jonah 3:10).

When Jonah saw that God was responding in mercy, he "was greatly displeased and became angry" (Jonah 4:1). God rebuked Jonah's reaction, demonstrating His compassion on those who are ignorant: "But Nineveh has more than a hundred and twenty thousand people who cannot tell their right hand from their left, and many cattle as well. Should I not be concerned about that great city?" (Jonah 4:11).

We must remember, then, that God's grace extends to those who are uninformed. This principle certainly applies to those who are wealthy. As Peter reminds us in his second letter, God is patient, "not wanting *anyone* to perish, but *everyone* to come to repentance" (2 Peter 3:9).

4. Being Open to Unique Opportunities

The next example we encounter in the book of Acts illustrates God's grace in the life of an Ethiopian eunuch. God gave Philip specific instructions to leave Samaria and head south toward Gaza to meet this man who was "an important official in charge of *all the treasury* of Candace, queen of the Ethiopians" (Acts 8:27). The eunuch was a black Gentile from Africa. He had developed a definite interest in the God of Abraham, Isaac, and Jacob. That is why he "had gone to Jerusalem to worship" (Acts 8:27*b*). It is also why he was reading from Isaiah the prophet (Acts 8:32-33). When Philip explained the gospel, this prominent and wealthy man responded immediately in repentance and faith and asked to be baptized (Acts 8:36-38).

Why did the Holy Spirit inspire Luke to record this event? It seems obvious that God wants us to know that wealthy people can and do respond to the gospel. This story adds balance to Christ's encounter with the rich young ruler.

Think of the influence this man had throughout his country once he returned to his homeland. That is one reason God wants us to reach these people. *They can influence great segments of humanity for Christ with both their social position and their material resources* (SCP 45).

5. Understanding God's Heart of Compassion

When the gospel began to penetrate the Gentile world, the Holy Spirit gave us another dramatic example to teach us an important truth regarding evangelizing wealthy people. God wants us to know that *His heart responds to non-Christians who are not only sincerely seeking to please Him but who express their sincerity through generosity with their material possessions* (SCP 50).

GOD'S COMPASSION TOWARD CORNELIUS

This principle is illustrated in the life of Cornelius, a Roman official who lived in Caesarea. Luke's historical record is pointed. God was uniquely drawn to this man because "he and all his family were *devout and God-fearing.*" Furthermore, the specific way he demonstrated this devotedness to God was that "he gave *generously to those in need* and prayed to God regularly" (Acts 10:2). Because this unsaved man was sincerely seeking to please God, evidently because of what he had seen in the lives of "God-fearing Jews" who lived in Caesarea, God sovereignly brought him in touch with Peter, who explained the gospel to him. Cornelius and his whole household responded in faith (Acts 10:1-48).

GOD'S COMPASSION TOWARD LYDIA

We see another example of this principle in Philippi on Paul's second missionary journey. Though there were not enough Jewish men in this Gentile city to form a synagogue, a group of "God-fearing women" gathered for prayer by a river outside the city gate. On a particular Sabbath day, Paul and the other members of his missionary team also went to this place of prayer "and began to speak to the women who had gathered there" (Acts 16:13).

"Lydia, a dealer in purple cloth from the city of Thyatira," was among them. She, too, "was a worshiper of God," though she did not know Christ personally. While listening to Paul preach the gospel, the Lord opened her heart, and she responded to the message of salvation (Acts 16:14-15). Immediately upon becoming a Christian, Lydia unselfishly opened her home to Paul, Silas, Timothy, and Luke. The church that was born that day in Philippi probably continued to meet in her home.

God sovereignly brings Christians in touch with unsaved people—in the case of Cornelius and Lydia, wealthy people who are searching for Him and who are demonstrating their sincerity with their acts of worship. Again, this does not teach salvation by works. This principle simply indicates that God's heart responds to people who are sincerely seeking to know Him and who are attempting to please Him.

There are multitudes of people like Cornelius and Lydia, particularly in American culture, who regularly come in contact with biblical Christianity. One of the challenges that faces us is to expose these people to our own worship experiences with God, including the way we use our material possessions. Once their hearts begin to respond with a desire to please God based upon what they have seen and heard, it will open the door to clearly explain the gospel—that we are saved by grace through faith and not by works (Ephesians 2:8-9).

6. Warning Materialistic Unbelievers

What we see in the lives of people like Simon the sorcerer, the Ethiopian eunuch, Cornelius, and Lydia leads us to another important principle. Though God's heart responds to non-Christians who are sincerely seeking to please Him and who express their sincerity through being generous with their material possessions, *we must warn them that to put their faith in material possessions will not bring eternal life.* Furthermore, when they become obsessed with those possessions, so much so that they abuse and misuse other people to accumulate wealth, *God will eventually judge them severely* (SCP 59).

No New Testament writer spoke to this issue more directly than James. His message was loud and clear. "Now listen, you rich people, weep and wail because of the misery that is coming upon you" (James 5:1).

James taught that material things do not provide ultimate happiness. Second, he taught that they are not enduring. They "rot." Even our finest clothes deteriorate. James wrote that even "gold and silver" will corrode or "rust" (James 5:2-3). Gold and silver that is hoarded will testify against us and eat our "flesh like fire" (James 5:3).

We must never compromise the message of salvation when communicating with unsaved people who are wealthy. They must understand that their wealth will never get them to heaven—no matter how benevolent they are. Furthermore, they must understand that the more they abuse people in their accumulation of wealth, the greater their judgment will be in eternity.

7. BEING WILLING TO TAKE RISKS

Philemon, another wealthy man who came to Christ in Colossae, illustrates that Christians who put God first in their lives may open the door for people to take advantage of them. When he became a Christian, he attempted to apply Christian principles immediately in the use of his material possessions. First, he took Paul's instructions seriously to treat his servants as fellow believers, as brothers and sisters in Jesus Christ (see Ephesians 6:5; Colossians 3:22–4:1). But one of his young slaves named Onesimus did not respond to the gospel of Christ. Furthermore, he took advantage of his new freedom and new relationship with his master. Not only did he escape from Philemon's household, but he evidently took some of Philemon's possessions with him (Philemon 18).

That doesn't sound like a happy story, but it ends beautifully. Onesimus showed up in Rome and came in contact with Paul while the apostle was in prison. Paul led him to a personal relationship with Jesus Christ and taught him the Word of God. Eventually Paul sent him back to his master—now as a brother in Christ.

The lesson in this fascinating story is clear. *If we are given to hospitality as God says we should be, there will always be people who abuse our generosity* (SCP 99). That should not surprise us. There are always risks in obeying Jesus Christ.

This does not mean that we should purposely and naively allow people to take advantage of us. But we must realize that when we obey God, such things will happen, no matter how hard we try to avoid it. The story of Onesimus certainly illustrates that doing the will of God is worth the risk.

8. BEING WILLING TO ENDURE CRITICISM

In extreme cases, *Christians may face criticism or even retaliation when their commitment to do God's will interferes with the materialistic desires of the unsaved world* (SCP 102). This is dramatically demonstrated when Paul went to Ephesus, a large center for idolatrous worship in the

Asian world. As always, idolatry and materialism go hand-in-glove. During a two-year period, while Paul was preaching and teaching in the lecture hall of Tyrannus, many people responded to the gospel and gave up their idolatrous activities. In fact, Paul's ministry was so effective that it began to cut into the profits of the idol business.

Demetrius, "who made silver shrines of Artemis," became so angry that he called a meeting of all those who were involved in similar businesses. "Men, you know we receive a good income from this business," Demetrius declared. "There is danger that not only our trade will lose its good name, but also that the temple of the great goddess Artemis will be discredited" (Acts 19:24-27a).

Though Demetrius disguised his motives by referring to his pagan religious convictions, his main concern was his pocketbook. As a result of this meeting, a serious riot broke out, and if the city clerk had not stepped in to calm the crowd, Paul could have been killed (Acts 19:35-41).

Over the centuries people have not changed in their hearts. Any time the message of Christianity cuts across the sinful practices of non-Christians and threatens their income, Christians can expect to be ridiculed, criticized, and even ostracized. Some believers actually lose their jobs because they refuse to participate in dishonest business practices. In some instances, unusual pressure is exerted by non-Christian business associates because an honest, conscientious, and industrious person in the organization makes everyone else "look bad."

Paul's experience in Ephesus illustrates that doing the will of God in relationship to our material possessions will involve risk. Fortunately, the positive experiences usually outweigh the negative ones. As we have seen, this was true even in the New Testament pagan world. The principles we have looked at in these two chapters support this conclusion.

LET'S CHECK OURSELVES

On a scale of one to ten, circle the number that best represents how well you believe the people in your church or group practice the biblical principle found in each question.

1. Does the affluence in our community make it difficult for those in our church to reach people with the gospel?

VERY LITTLE   SOMEWHAT   EXTENSIVELY

1   2   3   4   5   6   7   8   9   10

2. Do the leaders in our church understand business philosophy and structures in our larger community and use this knowledge to build spiritual

bridges to the economic community and communicate spiritual truths to them?

VERY LITTLE SOMEWHAT EXTENSIVELY

1 2 3 4 5 6 7 8 9 10

3. Are there self-serving people in our church who are taking advantage of God's patience and grace?

VERY LITTLE SOMEWHAT EXTENSIVELY

1 2 3 4 5 6 7 8 9 10

4. Are those in our church impacting people of prominence and wealth by reaching them with the gospel and in turn enabling these people to impact their own peers with the message of salvation?

VERY LITTLE SOMEWHAT EXTENSIVELY

1 2 3 4 5 6 7 8 9 10

5. Are the Christians in our church in loving and caring contact with unsaved people who are basically God-fearing and unselfish but who need to come to know Jesus Christ personally?

VERY LITTLE SOMEWHAT EXTENSIVELY

1 2 3 4 5 6 7 8 9 10

6. Has our church developed a way to sensitively communicate with unbelievers in our community that putting their faith and hope in material possessions will ultimately lead to disillusionment in this life and separation from God in the next?

VERY LITTLE SOMEWHAT EXTENSIVELY

1 2 3 4 5 6 7 8 9 10

7. Are Christians in our church willing to risk being taken advantage of, as it pertains to their material possessions, in order to be obedient to God?

VERY LITTLE SOMEWHAT EXTENSIVELY

1 2 3 4 5 6 7 8 9 10

8. Are Christians in our church, but especially our spiritual leaders, willing to face criticism and even retaliation from materialistically minded people because they are committed to teaching and practicing what God says about material possessions?

VERY LITTLE SOMEWHAT EXTENSIVELY

1 2 3 4 5 6 7 8 9 10

How to Use This Evaluation Exercise

1. Duplicate these eight questions on a separate sheet, and have each person in your group anonymously evaluate your church.
2. Tabulate the responses to find an average score. To do so, total the numbers circled in each question. Divide this total number by the number of people responding to that particular question. This will give you a "mean," or average, score.
3. Discover the greatest needs in your church by arranging the scores numerically from the highest to the lowest. Those scores that are lowest represent the areas that need immediate attention.
4. In discussing these scores and the principles involved, spend time first of all reviewing the areas of strength in your church. Spend time in prayer, thanking God for those strengths.
5. Finally, spend time discussing ways to practice the principles that are the most neglected in your church. The following questions will help:
   a. What are the areas of greatest need?
   b. What can we do that we are not doing to practice these biblical principles?
   c. What specific goals can we set up to practice these principles?
   d. What can we do *immediately*?

Personalize This Project

Follow the procedure described at the end of chapter 1.

3

Creating and Maintaining Love and Unity

Christians who view and use their material possessions in harmony with the will of God often cause others to understand and accept the message of the gospel. However, Scripture also illustrates and experience verifies that, when Christians obey God in this area of their lives, it also has a profound unifying effect on the Body of Christ.

1. ACHIEVING ONENESS

The way the Christians in Jerusalem used their material possessions certainly *reflected* their love and unity. But these acts of kindness also *created* more love and unity. Thus, as the church grew numerically and spiritually, sharing their material possessions to care for the physical needs of the people of God, "all the believers were one in heart and mind" (Acts 4:32).

Being selfish with material possessions breeds disunity—not harmony. Paul had to deal with this problem in the Corinthian church regarding the way these Christians were practicing the "agape," or "love feast" (1 Corinthians 11:17-33; Jude 12). This special meal was an extension of what Jesus instituted in the upper room (Matthew 26:26-30) and what the Jerusalem Christians practiced daily as "they broke bread in their homes and ate together with glad and sincere hearts" (Acts 2:46b).

As the Corinthians came together to share in this common meal and to remember the broken body and shed blood of Christ, some of the more affluent brought large portions of food and drink, and then proceeded to partake before others arrived. When the poor came with their more limited contributions, most of the food and drink had already been consumed. In fact, some of the more indulgent Corinthians were actually drunk (1 Corinthians 11:21). Paul was not happy with the situation: "In the following directives I have no praise for you, for your meetings do more harm than good. In the first place, I hear that when you come together as a church, there are *divisions* among you" (1 Corinthians 11:17-18).

The Corinthian illustration stands in sharp contrast to what happened in the first church. Believers in Jerusalem were "one in heart and mind." Their unselfish behavior in sharing their material possessions strongly contributed to this love and unity. By contrast, the Corinthians were divided and carnal because of their selfishness.

A clear principle emerges from these biblical examples. *When Christians use their material possessions to meet one another's needs, as God says we should, it will create love and unity in the Body of Christ* (SCP 2). In turn, this love and unity becomes a supernatural and powerful means of God to convince people that the gospel message is true. Jesus Christ prayed specifically for this dynamic to take place among Christians of all time: "May they be brought to complete unity *to let the world know that you sent me* and have loved them even as you have loved me" (John 17:23).

2. SEEKING FORGIVENESS

Jesus said, "If you are offering your gift at the altar and there remember that your brother has something against you, leave your gift there in front of the altar. First, go and be reconciled to your brother; then come and offer your gift" (Matthew 5:23-24). Jesus was illustrating the interrelatedness of the two great commandments, which are foundational for all the commandments. The "first and greatest" is that we should fervently love the Lord our God. The second is that we should love our neighbors as ourselves (Matthew 22:37-39).

Jesus' teachings set the stage for creating and maintaining love and unity in the Body of Christ. Applied to giving, Jesus taught His followers that, before they offered their material possessions to God, they must seek forgiveness from those they have wronged. To be out of harmony with their fellow Jews was to be out of harmony with God. Under these conditions, their gifts were not acceptable no matter what the size or how perfect they were. Without reconciliation, their "love for God" was marred because of their "lack of love for their neighbor."

Does this mean that the gifts these people offered at the altar were not accepted by God unless they had righted every wrong they had ever committed toward others? No. That would have put them—and us—in an impossible situation. Rather, Jesus was teaching that *when we harbor conscious memories of sin against another Christian and have not asked forgiveness, we are to do all we can to be at peace with that person before continuing to offer material possessions to the Lord* (SCP 22). Just as the apostle Paul exhorted the Corinthians to examine themselves before they participated in eating and drinking at the Lord's Supper (1 Corinthians 11:27-29), so we are to examine ourselves when we worship God with our material gifts. If we discover that we have sinned against a fellow Christian, we should seek forgiveness as soon as possible.

The apostle Paul affirmed this principle in his letter to the Romans. When exhorting all Christians to pay whatever they owe—taxes, revenue, respect, honor—Paul concluded with this specific, yet general, admonition: "Let no debt remain outstanding, except the continuing debt to love one another" (Romans 13:7-8). Paul is elaborating on what he had stated earlier: "If it is possible, as far as it depends on you, live at peace with everyone" (Romans 12:18), including those who are not Christians.

3. Avoiding Invalidation in Our Giving

Jesus extended this concept of having right relationships with God and others when He addressed the teachers of the law and Pharisees in Matthew 23. Referring to the laws of God regarding tithing, as outlined in the Old Testament (Luke 27:30-33; Deuteronomy 14:22-29), He in essence accused these men of "straining out a gnat" while swallowing "a camel" (Matthew 23:24). These religious leaders were giving a tenth of the small aromatic herbs from their gardens—actually going beyond the requirements given in the law of Moses. But they were presenting to God what was easy to grow and easy to give—and even being arrogant about it. At the same time, they were not practicing the more important aspects of the law—justice, mercy, and faithfulness (Matthew 23:23).

When we principlize from what Jesus was teaching these religious leaders of His day, He is simply telling Christians of all time that *even if we give regularly and faithfully, we are invalidating the acceptability of our gifts when we neglect to love God and one another* (SCP 34). This certainly includes our ethical conduct. Some Christians seem to believe that if they give sizable amounts of money to God's work, this benevolent act compensates for the unethical way in which they have made that money. Not so, said Jesus. Being generous will never compensate for dishonesty and insensitivity. Furthermore, generous giving will never cancel out the results of a life-style that conforms to this world's system. God wants us to do His will in all respects (Romans 12:1-2).

4. Winning Respect and Love

When Paul wrote to the Corinthians, he underscored the fact that *Christians respect and have a special love for fellow Christians who are unselfish and generous* (SCP 86). He spoke of the Jewish Christians in Judea who would receive their gifts: "And in their prayers for you, *their hearts will go out to you*, because of the surpassing grace [of giving] God has given you" (2 Corinthians 9:14).

It has often been said that people cannot hate people who truly love. So it can also be said that people usually cannot continue to resent Christians who are unselfish and generous with their material possessions. Just as the generosity among Gentile Christians in the first-century world broke down the theological and cultural barriers that existed because of Jewish prejudice (Romans 15:27), Christians who are unselfish and generous in the twentieth-century world will also break down the social and cultural barriers that exist among Christ's followers. Generally speaking, people do respect and love Christians who are unselfish and generous.

5. Showing Appreciation to Faithful Givers

The principle of showing appreciation to individuals, as well as to groups of Christians, who are faithful in sharing their material possessions can be demonstrated throughout the New Testament. The apostles changed Joseph's name to Barnabas to acknowledge his generous spirit (Acts 4:36-37). Paul wrote to Philemon: "Your love has given me great joy and encouragement, because you, brother, have refreshed the hearts of the saints" (Philemon 7). Most Bible interpreters agree that Paul was referring to the way Philemon utilized his wealth, and particularly his home, to show Christian hospitality.

Paul showed appreciation to a *group* of Christians when he wrote to the Corinthians. Referring to the Macedonian churches, he said, "We want you to know about the grace that God has given" to these churches. "Out of the most severe trial, their overflowing joy and their extreme poverty welled up in rich generosity. For I testify that they gave as much as they were able, and even beyond their ability" (2 Corinthians 8:2-3).

Today, *Christian leaders need to develop sensitive but specific ways to show appreciation to Christians for being faithful, not only with their time and talents but with their treasures* (SCP 7, 108). All Christians, both individually and corporately, need this kind of encouragement.

6. Accepting Our High Position in Christ

In the Body of Christ every member is important. This is a straightforward teaching throughout the New Testament (see 1 Corinthians 12:21-23). Certainly, among other things, the social and economic status of individual Christians is included in this principle. That is the way the Lord designed the church to function. Just because people do not have a lot of material possessions does not mean that they are insignificant.

True, one of God's unique gifts for the church include people like Cornelius, Philemon, and Lydia, who used their wealth to carry out the Great Commission. But people like Peter and John and Dorcas are also God's unique gifts to the church. They did not have "silver and gold," but they gave what they had (Acts 3:6). James, more than any other New Testament writer, gives us specific guidelines as to how to maintain unity in the Body of Christ no matter what our economic status.

James asserts that "the brother in humble circumstances ought to take pride in his high position" (James 1:9). Many poor people became Christians in the New Testament world. In spite of their constant hope that Jesus would soon return to restore the kingdom to Israel and reign and rule as their Messiah, these believers discovered rather quickly that following Jesus Christ did not automatically solve their economic problems. Those who became Christians in the midst of "humble circumstances" often remained in humble circumstances the rest of their lives. They knew nothing of the "prosperity theology" that is so frequently taught today in the more affluent cultures of the world.[1]

One major thing did change, however. They had a new perspective on life. They had *eternal hope.* Thus, James was writing to encourage anyone in "humble circumstances . . . to take pride in his *high position*" (James 1:9). What they lacked materially had nothing to do with their "high position in Christ." They may not have had much by this world's standards, but they were exceedingly rich in God's sight. They were "heirs of God and co-heirs with Christ" (Romans 8:17).

Poor Christians, then, are just as "rich" as well-to-do Christians in terms of the way God views their position in His church (SCP 53). Consequently spiritual leaders have a responsibility to encourage these believers not to be intimidated by more well-to-do believers. But neither must Christians with fewer material possessions judge, criticize, or question the motives of more affluent Christians.

7. Demonstrating Humility

James also directed some straightforward words to affluent Christians: "But the one who is rich should take pride in his low position, because he will pass away like a wild flower" (James 1:10). James was cautioning wealthy people to let others see that their riches were not the most important thing in life. They were to let people know that their eternal perspective was far more important than their earthly one. If they should die at any moment (their "low position"), it would be clear that their primary security was in Jesus Christ and in their hope of eternal life.

Christians, then, who have a lot of material possessions should demonstrate humility, realizing that their only true treasures are those they have stored up in heaven (SCP 54). Today we need to understand this principle, particularly those of us who live in materialistic and affluent cultures. Without even being aware of it, we can easily convey an attitude of arrogance and superiority. When we do, we destroy unity in the Body of Christ rather than create it.

Again, a word of caution is in order for Christians who may not have as much as others. People who are insecure and jealous because of their lack can become very critical of affluent Christians and can falsely accuse them of pride and materialism. It is easy to project on others what might possibly be true of us if we had more of this world's goods. At this juncture, Paul's words to the Roman Christians are apropos: "Therefore, let us stop passing judgment on one another. Instead, make up your mind not to put any stumbling block or obstacle in your brother's way" (Romans 14:13).

8. Avoiding Favoritism

The Bible teaches that we are to give honor to whom honor is due—including those who are faithful in serving God with their material possessions. Barnabas and Philemon are classic illustrations of men who were so honored. However, while honoring some, we must not dishonor others. We must never allocate the poor to a lower position because of their economic conditions. This, James stated, is terribly wrong and sinful. It is discriminating and out of harmony with our Christian faith.

To get his point across, James used an illustration:

> Suppose a man comes into your meeting wearing a gold ring and fine clothes, and a poor man in shabby clothes also comes in. If you show special attention to the man wearing fine clothes and say, "Here's a good seat for you," but say to the poor man, "You stand there" or "Sit on the floor by my feet," have you not discriminated among yourselves and become judges with evil thoughts? (James 2:2-4)

God does not discriminate. Therefore, *we must not show favoritism to those who have an abundance of material possessions* (SCP 56). Some believers who have had the least in the "kingdom of this world" will be exceedingly wealthy in the "kingdom of God." They may be poor in material possessions, but they are rich in faith. Since God treats all Christians equally as heirs and joint heirs with Jesus Christ, so should we.

Note

1. See the first part of chapters 7 and 8 for further discussion of prosperity theology. Also see Michael Horton, ed., *The Agony of Deceit: What Some TV Preachers Are Really Teaching* (Chicago: Moody, 1990); Bruce Barron, *The Health and Wealth Gospel: A Fresh Look at Healing, Prosperity & Positive Confession* (Downers Grove, Ill.: InterVarsity, 1987).

LET'S CHECK OURSELVES

On a scale of one to ten, circle the number that best represents how well you believe the people in your church or group practice the biblical principle found in each question.

1. Are love and unity discernible in our church because believers are using their material possessions to meet one another's needs?

VERY LITTLE				SOMEWHAT				EXTENSIVELY	
1	2	3	4	5	6	7	8	9	10

2. Do people in our church make an effort to have a clear conscience in their relationships with other Christians so that their gifts are acceptable to God?

VERY LITTLE				SOMEWHAT				EXTENSIVELY	
1	2	3	4	5	6	7	8	9	10

3. Do the people in our church clearly understand that their gifts are acceptable to God to the degree they love God and their brothers and sisters in Christ?

VERY LITTLE				SOMEWHAT				EXTENSIVELY	
1	2	3	4	5	6	7	8	9	10

4. Do the believers in our church accept the fact that it is by divine design that faithful givers will generate love and respect from other believers?

VERY LITTLE				SOMEWHAT				EXTENSIVELY	
1	2	3	4	5	6	7	8	9	10

5. Do we have a sensitive system and approach in our church for showing special appreciation to those who are faithful in sharing their material possessions?

VERY LITTLE				SOMEWHAT				EXTENSIVELY	
1	2	3	4	5	6	7	8	9	10

6. Do most Christians in our church who do not have a lot of material possessions feel comfortable and accepted?

VERY LITTLE				SOMEWHAT				EXTENSIVELY	
1	2	3	4	5	6	7	8	9	10

7. Do affluent Christians in our church demonstrate true humility in their relationships with fellow believers who do not have as much of this world's goods?

VERY LITTLE				SOMEWHAT				EXTENSIVELY	
1	2	3	4	5	6	7	8	9	10

8. Are the Christians in our church free from showing favoritism to affluent people and at the same time free from prejudice against the poor?

VERY LITTLE				SOMEWHAT				EXTENSIVELY	
1	2	3	4	5	6	7	8	9	10

How to Use This Evaluation Exercise

1. Duplicate these eight questions on a separate sheet, and have each person in your group anonymously evaluate your church.
2. Tabulate the responses to find an average score. To do so, total the numbers circled in each question. Divide this total number by the number of people responding to that particular question. This will give you a "mean," or average, score.
3. Discover the greatest needs in your church by arranging the scores numerically from the highest to the lowest. Those scores that are lowest represent the areas that need immediate attention.
4. In discussing these scores and the principles involved, spend time first of all reviewing the areas of strength in your church. Spend time in prayer, thanking God for those strengths.
5. Finally, spend time discussing ways to practice the principles that are the most neglected in your church. The following questions will help:
   a. What are the areas of greatest need?
   b. What can we do that we are not doing to practice these biblical principles?
   c. What specific goals can we set up to practice these principles?
   d. What can we do *immediately*?

Personalize This Project

Follow the procedure described at the end of chapter 1.

4

The Power of Modeling

Demonstrating and illustrating what Christianity is all about has been a part of God's communication strategy since the beginning of this great and dynamic movement. This is what Jesus had in mind when He said to His disciples, "All men will know you are my disciples if you love one another" (John 13:35). This is also why there is so much emphasis throughout the New Testament letters on the importance of modeling God's will to others. It should not surprise us, then, that the same principle is illustrated again and again in the way Christians should view and use their material possessions.

1. GOD'S PLAN FOR MODELING: SPIRITUAL LEADERS

Modeling a sacrificial spirit began with the apostles in Jerusalem. They stood out immediately as men who were willing to give up the accumulation of material possessions to serve Jesus Christ and His kingdom. In fact, Peter, when asked for a contribution by the crippled beggar in the Temple, responded by saying that he and John had no "silver or gold" (Acts 3:6). This was literally true. Both men had given up what probably was a rather productive fishing business to follow Christ and "fish for men" instead. All of the other apostles, in one way or another, had followed suit. Their example was dynamic and powerful. They never asked others to do what they had not done themselves.

As local churches were established, elders were appointed to carry on the ministry as spiritual leaders. The Scriptures make clear that "eldership" and generosity are corollary concepts. Conversely, being a local church leader and being selfish are incompatible. The people these leaders serve should be able to look to them as godly models in the use of their material possessions.

Peter underscored this principle in his first letter. "Be shepherds of God's flock that is under your care," he wrote to the elders. These leaders were not to be "greedy for money," but eager to serve. They were not to lord it over those who had been entrusted to them. Rather, they were to be "*examples* to the flock" (1 Peter 5:1-3).

Modeling in the area of giving is not only a New Testament principle. David shared in detail with "the whole assembly" what he had decided to give to help build the Temple (1 Chronicles 28:1), from both his corporate resources as king of Israel and from his personal resources (1 Chronicles 29:2-5). Consequently, those listening were so encouraged that they, in turn, "gave willingly . . . toward the work on the temple of God" (1 Chronicles 29:6-7). Furthermore, this "leadership model" impacted all Israel, for "the people rejoiced at the *willing response* of their leaders, for they had given *freely* and *wholeheartedly* to the Lord" (1 Chronicles 29:9).

God's people today also need visible leadership models (SCP 3, 113). How this "fleshes out" methodologically will vary greatly in different cultural circumstances. What must be consistent in every situation, however, is the "model" itself.

2. God's Plan for Modeling: Fellow Believers

An insistence on total confidentiality in giving contradicts the examples in the Word of God. No one can deny that what Barnabas did was visible, not only to the apostles but to many other Christians in Jerusalem. Otherwise, Ananias and Sapphira would not have attempted to do the same thing, but with wrong motives.

Christians today—just as the Christians in the New Testament era— *need both leadership examples and the example of fellow believers to inspire them to use their material possessions to further the work of the kingdom of God* (SCP 8). Mere verbal teaching alone will not motivate this action. It is true that Jesus said on one occasion, "But when you give to the needy, do not let your left hand know what your right hand is doing, so that your giving may be in secret" (Matthew 6:3-4). We will see, however, that His statement does not contradict this principle. (See chapter 6 for what Jesus really meant by this statement.)

3. God's Plan for Modeling: The Nation Israel

Those who composed the first church were, for the most part, Jews who took their religion very seriously. This was particularly true of the visitors in Jerusalem at the time the church was founded. Luke stated that those who "were staying in Jerusalem" at the time of the Holy Spirit's coming on the Day of Pentecost were "*God-fearing* Jews from every nation under heaven" (Acts 2:5). Great numbers of these "Grecian Jews," along with many from the "Aramaic-speaking community" (residents of Jerusalem and Judea), became believers (Acts 6:1).

To be "God-fearing Jews" simply meant that these people were committed to doing everything they could to keep the Old Testament laws. We can certainly assume that most of them, before they became Christians, practiced the Old Testament regulations regarding tithing. When God called Israel out of Egypt and gave them the law at Mount Sinai, He basically instituted a three-tithe system.

The first tithe involved one-tenth of all yearly produce and one-tenth of all the flocks and cattle. This tithe was to be used to support the Levites and priests as they spiritually ministered to Israel (Leviticus 27:30-34).

The second tithe, also known as the "festival tithe," was one-tenth of the nine-tenths left after the first tithe was given. This tithe was to be set apart and taken to Jerusalem. If it was impossible to make the trip with produce and animals, a tenth of their possessions could be sold. The money could be used to make the trip and then to purchase food or animals for offerings in Jerusalem (Deuteronomy 12:5-7; 14:22-27).

The third tithe, sometimes identified as the "charity tithe," was given during the third year. It was to be designated for Levites, strangers, the fatherless, and those who were widowed (Deuteronomy 26:12; 14:28-29).[1]

In addition to these tithes, faithful Jews also paid a Temple tax (referred to when collectors approached Peter and asked if Jesus paid this tax). Matthew, a former tax collector, identified this amount as "the two drachma" tax (Matthew 17:24). Under the Romans, of course, the Jews also paid various taxes to the Roman government, both within the empire and in the local areas.

When these "God-fearing Jews" became Christians, they not only paid taxes to the Roman government, but it is safe to assume that they naturally transferred their economic loyalty from Judaism to Christianity. It is no wonder that we see such generous people among these Christians in Jerusalem. They were in the habit of giving regularly and systematically. It was a part of their religious training and commitment. Furthermore, when they understood the grace of God in comparison with being under law, it appears that they not only calculated tenths, but on occasions, generously gave the total profits from the sale of certain properties. In this sense, the principle of "grace giving" at times led these new believers to exceed what the law required in the Old Testament.

Though the tithe system is never mentioned in the New Testament, it certainly influenced these Jewish Christians. Church history reveals that these Old Testament giving patterns influenced the Gentile community as pagans also became Christians. *Though the tithe laws were never perpetuated in Christianity as they were in the Old Testament, they serve as a model to Christians for regular and systematic giving* (SCP 20). We cannot ignore this model when we evaluate Paul's instructions to the Corinthians: "On the first day of every week, each one of you should set aside a sum of money in keeping with his income" (1 Corinthians 16:2). Nor should we ignore this Old Testament model when determining how much we should give as Christians.

4. GOD'S PLAN FOR MODELING: LOCAL CHURCHES

Every local Body of believers needs the real-life examples of other churches as positive models in the area of giving (SCP 70). Paul illustrated this principle in his second letter to the Corinthians. Initially these Achaian believers seemed to think they were doing rather well in sharing their material possessions. After all, their eager response to the financial needs of the poor Christians in Jerusalem had motivated the Macedonian Christians to participate (2 Corinthians 9:2). However, the Corinthians had not matched their "walk" with their "talk."

In an ironic reversal, Paul used the Macedonian churches as a positive model for the Corinthians (2 Corinthians 8:1-5, 8). Thus, he began chapter 8 with these words: "And now, brothers, we want you to know about the grace God has given the Macedonian churches."

Paul went on to remind the Corinthians that the believers in these churches had given generously in the midst of a very difficult situation. In fact, Paul used the phrase "extreme poverty" to identify their economic circumstances. Yet they gave with "overflowing joy" and with "rich generosity" (2 Corinthians 8:2).

This kind of giving is not something God demands from His children. He is aware that we have basic needs, and nowhere in Scripture are Christians commanded to give away what is necessary for their own existence. God wants us to use wisdom in preparing for circumstances beyond our control. But the believers in Macedonia seemed to ignore these factors, both as it related to their present circumstances and to future emergencies. They gave beyond what may be considered "common sense."

Furthermore, the Macedonian Christians were not responding to coercion. Paul may have even cautioned them against this kind of sacrificial giving. But "entirely on their own," they responded by "urgently pleading" with Paul and his fellow missionaries to be able to do something for other Christians in need (2 Corinthians 8:3-4). Consequently they became a model of sacrificial giving.

The principle of "local church modeling" deserves special attention, particularly in affluent areas of the world. Many in the American church have no concept of sacrificial giving. And yet there are groups of Christians in Third World countries that are "Macedonian" in nature. They are giving out of poverty, while most of us give out of plenty. We need to know about these believers. It will help activate many of us to greater commitment.

I was deeply impressed with the story of a small struggling church in northern Chile. Most of the believers were very poor with large families. It was not uncommon for parents to send a child to the store to buy one egg and two potatoes. Initially, the monthly offerings in the church totaled no more than six dollars.

A missionary involved in planting this church was concerned about the financial condition of this small body of Christians. How could he help them become self-supporting and indigenous? He began to pray about the matter.

About six weeks later, the missionary stopped to visit a middle-aged couple who had recently become Christians. They had begun reading the Bible on their own and had discovered the concept of "tithing." They began to ask questions. It did not occur to the missionary initially that this was an answer to his prayers. In fact, he tried to dodge the question. The man was a carpenter and had been without work for months. He and his wife had somehow managed to care for themselves and their twenty-five Rhode Island Red hens on the income from the eggs laid each day. He was certain it would be a waste of time to talk to them about "tithing."

But this couple would not be denied. So the missionary showed them the classic passages regarding regular and systematic giving in 1 Corinthians 16 and 2 Corinthians 8–9. The rest of the story is remarkable. It is one that every American church needs to know about. It is an exciting and inspiring example.

> The following Sunday at the end of the meeting, Manuel handed me an envelope. When he saw the puzzled look on my face, he said with a note of pride, "That's our tithe!"
>
> I could scarcely believe it and stood for a long moment with the envelope in my hand. When he had gone, I opened the flap and saw two or three small bills equaling about 19 cents.
>
> The next Sunday afternoon I was passing their house on my bicycle when they waved me down. They had some exciting news. The Tuesday morning after they had given their tithe, there wasn't a crumb of bread in the house for breakfast, nor money to buy more.
>
> Their first impulse was to take the few pesos that had accumulated in the tithe box. But on second thought, Manuel said, "No, we won't. That's God's money. We will go without breakfast this morning."
>
> There wasn't anything to do but attend to the chickens. Much to their amazement, several of the hens had already laid eggs—at 6:30 in the morning! Never before had they laid before noon.
>
> They gathered up the eggs, and Manuel hurried to the corner store. Eggs brought a good price, so he came back with enough bread for the entire day.
>
> That same afternoon, a little old man with a pushcart knocked on their door, asking if they might have any fertilizer to sell. They hadn't cleaned out the chicken house for some time, so they were able to gather 20 sackfuls.
>
> That, too, brought a good price. They bought feed for the hens, staple groceries for themselves—and had money left over.

They decided the wife should buy a pair of shoes with the extra money. The next afternoon, she got on a bus and rode 12 kilometers around the bay to a bigger town.

As soon as she got off the bus, she bumped into a nephew she had not seen for five years. They greeted each other affectionately, and he asked what she might be doing in his town. When she explained, he said, "Well, I've got a shoe store right behind you. Come on in and see what you can find."

She soon found just what she needed, at the exact price she dared spend. The nephew wrapped up the package, and she handed him the money. "Oh no, Aunt, I can't take your money. These shoes are a gift from me."

"No, no, Nephew! That wouldn't be right. Please take the money."

When the argument ended, she found herself out in the street with both the shoes and the money.

The following week, Manuel got a job on a project that would last for two years. The workmen were paid every 15 days. And sure enough, after each payday, this couple arrived at church with their tithe, which now amounted to more than the offering of the rest of the congregation.

Word got around the church, and others began to experiment in giving. I had been paying the rent on the old building, along with the light and water bills, but soon there was money in the treasury to cover all three.

The congregation continued to grow, and so did the income. Each month our books showed more surplus in the treasury. I knew that one of the mission's national pastors working among the Indians was not receiving the support he needed and deserved, so I suggested that we designate some money for him. The congregation agreed, and we sent him the equivalent of $20 each month.

Before long, the church was ready to have its own pastor, and an invitation went to that same man. When he arrived, my wife and I were free to move to a new location and start another church.

The next two years brought continued good news. As the congregation continued to grow, they bought the old building and lots I had rented for them. They began remodeling, and soon they had an attractive, modern structure with Sunday school rooms and an auditorium seating 200.

On our last visit, they had just completed a house for the pastor, solidly built of cement blocks, with a living room-kitchen, bath, and four bedrooms, and they had started a branch church in a housing area a mile away.

We had offered up a little bit of prayer and 19 cents, and God did the rest.[2]

5. MODELING PROVIDES ENCOURAGEMENT

Can you imagine the encouragement Manuel and his wife were to this missionary? They were also a great encouragement to the total congregation. The Holy Spirit inspired Luke to record a marvelous example of this principle at work. We have already met Barnabas. His original name was Joseph, and he was a Levite from Cyprus who evidently had been in Jerusalem for some time. Either he had moved to Jerusalem permanently and invested in real estate or he operated his business from his home in Cyprus. Whatever the circumstances, this man owned land in Jerusalem, and when the need arose, he "sold a field that he owned and brought the money and put it at the apostles' feet" (Acts 4:37).

Though this man's name was Joseph, the apostles renamed him Barnabas, which means "Son of Encouragement." This fact alone tells us a great deal about how Barnabas viewed and used his material possessions. It also demonstrates that this kind of modeling encourages others.

More specifically, anyone who has ever been in Christian leadership and responsible for meeting the physical needs of others can identify with the reason the apostles changed Joseph's name to Barnabas. *People who are generous are special encouragers, not only to other Christians but to God Himself* (SCP 6). The church of Jesus Christ needs more people like Barnabas—and Manuel—who will encourage their Christian leaders, as well as others in the Body of Christ, to also be generous.

6. Modeling Motivates Others to Be Generous

When Paul first presented the special needs of the Christians in Jerusalem to the Corinthian believers, they responded enthusiastically. Though they had difficulty following through because of their own failure to plan their giving properly, the fact still remained that their "enthusiasm stirred" many of the Macedonian Christians to action (2 Corinthians 9:2).

The Corinthian model provides us with a dynamic principle. *Christians who are generous will motivate other Christians to be generous* (SCP 77). Many believers today have not been taught to give, or, if they have been taught, they are not yet responsive. They need to see other Christians enthusiastically using their material possessions to further the work of God's kingdom. They need to observe joyful giving so that they might respond with the same enthusiasm.

7. Modeling Generates a Desire to Worship God

Through us your generosity will result in *thanksgiving to God.* This service that you perform is not only supplying the needs of God's people but is also overflowing in many *expressions of thanks to God.* Because of the service by which you have proved yourselves, men will *praise God* for the obedience that accompanies your confession of the gospel of Christ, and for your generosity in sharing with them and with everyone else. (2 Corinthians 9:11b-13)

Paul reminded the Corinthians that not only would their generous gift meet the "needs of God's people" but it would also cause many people to praise God. People would thank God for these material blessings. They would also thank God for the Corinthians and the Macedonians and all of the other Christians who contributed to meet their needs. And they would thank and praise God for who He is.

The same principle applies today. *Generous Christians cause others to praise and worship God* (SCP 85). Nothing brings a more positive response than to see other believers being faithful stewards of their material possessions. Though it may create appropriate guilt in the lives of those who are not obeying God as they should, it will still bring a response of thanksgiving and praise in the hearts of those who want to respond to God's Spirit in all things.

NOTES

1. Jewish authorities differ in their opinion regarding the third tithe. Josephus indicates that it was offered every third year and was in addition to the first and second tithe. Others believe that every third year the second tithe (festival tithe) was given to the poor and needy in their local communities instead of taking it to Jerusalem.

2. Lyle Eggleston, "The Church That Learned to Give," *Moody Monthly* (July/August 1988), pp. 31-32.

LET'S CHECK OURSELVES

On a scale of one to ten, circle the number that best represents how well you believe the people in your church or group practice the biblical principle found in each question.

1. Are the spiritual leaders in our church modeling the way all Christians should use their material possessions?

VERY LITTLE				SOMEWHAT				EXTENSIVELY	
1	2	3	4	5	6	7	8	9	10

2. Do the people in our church have opportunity to observe other believers who are especially faithful in sharing their material possessions?

VERY LITTLE				SOMEWHAT				EXTENSIVELY	
1	2	3	4	5	6	7	8	9	10

3. Is God's Old Testament model used to challenge the people in our church to give regularly, systematically, and proportionately?

VERY LITTLE				SOMEWHAT				EXTENSIVELY	
1	2	3	4	5	6	7	8	9	10

4. Are people in our church exposed to other churches who are positive models in the area of giving?

VERY LITTLE				SOMEWHAT				EXTENSIVELY	
1	2	3	4	5	6	7	8	9	10

5. Are individual Christians encouraging others in our church with their generous acts of love?

VERY LITTLE				SOMEWHAT				EXTENSIVELY	
1	2	3	4	5	6	7	8	9	10

6. Does our church stand out as a model in motivating other churches to be generous with their material possessions?

VERY LITTLE				SOMEWHAT				EXTENSIVELY	
1	2	3	4	5	6	7	8	9	10

7. Do other Christians praise and worship God because the believers in our church are faithful in their giving?

VERY LITTLE				SOMEWHAT				EXTENSIVELY	
1	2	3	4	5	6	7	8	9	10

HOW TO USE THIS EVALUATION EXERCISE

1. Duplicate these seven questions on a separate sheet, and have each person in your group anonymously evaluate your church.
2. Tabulate the responses to find an average score. To do so, total the numbers circled in each question. Divide this total number by the number of people responding to that particular question. This will give you a "mean," or average, score.
3. Discover the greatest needs in your church by arranging the scores numerically from the highest to the lowest. Those scores that are lowest represent the areas that need immediate attention.
4. In discussing these scores and the principles involved, spend time first of all reviewing the areas of strength in your church. Spend time in prayer, thanking God for those strengths.
5. Finally, spend time discussing ways to practice the principles that are the most neglected in your church. The following questions will help:
   a. What are the areas of greatest need?
   b. What can we do that we are not doing to practice these biblical principles?
   c. What specific goals can we set up to practice these principles?
   d. What can we do *immediately*?

PERSONALIZE THIS PROJECT

Follow the procedure described at the end of chapter 1.

5

Meeting Human Needs

A predominant theme in Scripture is that Christians should share their material possessions to meet human needs. We are given a number of biblical guidelines that will help us respond appropriately in a variety of specific situations, including what to do when Christians attempt to take advantage of others.

1. MEETING SPECIAL NEEDS

The circumstances in Jerusalem were unique and unusual, and the Christians had special needs. So "from time to time those who owned lands or houses sold them, brought the money from the sales and put it at the apostles' feet, and it was distributed to anyone *as he had need*" (Acts 4:34-35).

This New Testament example illustrates an ongoing phenomenon throughout church history. There are always unusual circumstances that create special needs among God's people. In New Testament days it was sometimes a famine, such as the one faced by the Jerusalem Christians several years later. In this instance, the church in Antioch came to the rescue (Acts 11:25-30). Later, Paul faced special needs because of his imprisonment in Rome, and the Philippian church rose to the occasion and met his needs (Philippians 4:10-20).

And so it is today. *Special needs emerge, and when they do, God's people should respond to those needs* (SCP 4). Not to respond when it is possible to do so is to violate the will of God.

2. MEETING CONSISTENT NEEDS

Whereas there will always be unusual needs calling for special sacrifices, ordinary physical human needs are ongoing. Consequently, *consis-*

tent human needs should continue to be a primary factor promoting consistent giving (SCP 5).

In the New Testament, Christians are exhorted to care for the needs of those who minister to them spiritually (Galatians 6:10; 1 Timothy 5:17-19). They are also directed to care for the needs of their families (1 Timothy 5:8) and are given directives to meet the physical needs of the poor (1 Timothy 5:5; James 1:27). In fact, they are commanded to show hospitality to friends and strangers alike (Hebrews 13:2).

Interestingly, this is the same emphasis we see in the Old Testament. The first tithe was designated to meet the regular physical needs of those who were to minister to Israel spiritually. The second tithe was to care for family needs involved in making an annual trip to Jerusalem to worship God. And the third tithe was given to care for the needs of the poor, whom God says will always be among us.

Following the first two centuries A.D., Christians were eventually allowed to purchase property. They shared their own material possessions to construct buildings that would provide a place for the church to gather and worship God, just as God's Old Testament people did when they built the Temple and, later, the synagogues. This, too, was meeting a significant need—a corporate human need for a permanent place to gather together on a regular basis, not just to worship but to "encourage one another" (Hebrews 10:25).

Undergirding our motivation to meet human needs, of course, should always be our love for God. That should be the ultimate reason we share our material possessions. When we give to meet the needs of others, we are engaging in an act of worship. In other words, God accepts our love for our fellow human beings as an expression of our love for Him.

3. Caring for Parents

The Pharisees and teachers of the law had devised a set of rules whereby people could classify their material possessions as being "devoted to God" (Matthew 15:5-6). By making certain "religious decisions," the Jews were legally "freed up" from having to take care of their fathers and mothers. Sadly, the Pharisees had developed these traditions in order to keep more money for themselves.

Jesus directed some of His sharpest barbs toward this kind of hypocrisy. He told them in no uncertain terms that they had violated the law of God—which says that they must honor their fathers and mothers (Exodus 20:12). Paul reinforced what Jesus taught in his first letter to Timothy: "If anyone does not provide for his relatives, and especially for his immediate family, he has denied the faith and is worse than an unbeliever" (1 Timothy 5:8).

The principle God wants all of us to apply stands out boldly in Scripture. *Christian children who are able should make sure that they care for their parents' physical needs* (SCP 32). Not to do so is to seriously violate God's will.

Cultures, of course, vary in terms of economic structures that have been devised to care for people who have reached old age. In American society, we have retirement pensions, unemployment benefits, Social Security, Medicare, and senior citizen discounts. These private and governmental programs must, of course, be factored into the way we apply this biblical principle. If our parents' needs are being met in other ways, this enables us to utilize excess funds more creatively in caring for needs within the larger family—the church. But these governmental provisions for the elderly must never be used as a rationalization to neglect parents or to keep more for ourselves.

Conversely, applying this principle does not mean that we are to allow our parents to be selfish or to take advantage of us. But it does mean that we should assist our parents when they have bona fide needs—whether they are Christians or non-Christians. In fact, even if they are resentful of what we have and who we are, this should not be the deciding factor as to whether or not we help them.

4. Caring for the Poor

There are many ways to reflect our love for God. But James reminds us that nothing is more reflective of true religion than the way Christians care for the physical needs of children without parents and women without husbands: "Religion that God our Father accepts as pure and faultless is this: to look after orphans and widows in their distress" (James 1:27*a*).

This is not a new concern in God's overall plan. He designed the "third tithe" in Israel for this very purpose (Deuteronomy 14:28-29; 26:12). This continued to be an important focus in the New Testament church, since Jewish widows—once they became Christians—were cut off from the welfare system in Judaism.

God is concerned about the poor, and He notices Christians who share His concern by meeting these human needs. When Christians respond to meet needs with generous and open hearts, God accepts these acts of kindness as being "pure and faultless." To be sure, God keeps accurate records and will someday reward Christians who have been faithful in this respect. The principle is this: *People who are in physical need have a special place in God's heart.* Furthermore, *Christians who help meet these physical needs also have a special place in God's heart* (SCP 55).

5. HELPING PEOPLE IN CRISIS

The apostle Paul stated, "Our desire is not that others might be relieved while you are hard pressed, but that there might be equality" (2 Corinthians 8:13). With this statement, Paul was in no way advocating a socialist system where all share and share alike. Neither was he trying to make life difficult for the Corinthians while they were helping others. Rather, he was simply attempting to get them to help others who were in greater need than they. He was dealing with a specific situation in which Christians were experiencing unusual trials and were in deep economic need. He approached the Corinthians, because he knew they had more and could help those who had less. "Equality" here simply refers to mutual sharing in the midst of a crisis.

In the next verse, Paul explained why he asked the Corinthians to share with the Christians in Jerusalem: "At the present time, your plenty will supply what they need, so that in turn their plenty will supply what you need. Then there will be equality" (2 Corinthians 8:14).

The Corinthians were probably not as bad off as they thought. Paul addressed them as having "plenty" at this point in their lives—at least "plenty" in terms of what it would take to meet their own needs and still have some left to share with others who had a greater need than they.

Note also that what Paul was teaching the Corinthians was a temporary solution. All that he shared in his New Testament letters, especially with the Thessalonians, demonstrates that he wanted all Christians to be free from having to rely on others to meet their needs. On the other hand, Paul recognized that some needs would be ongoing—such as the needs of people who had no family to help them and who were unable to work because of age or illness.

But the whole of Scripture teaches that in the majority of situations, God's people will be able to work and earn their own living and "not be dependent on anybody" (1 Thessalonians 4:11-12). At times, however, Christians with resources should help those in need to once again be able to care for themselves. Putting it in principle form, *it is not the will of God that some Christians cannot meet their physical needs while other Christians with abundance could help them in their time of need* (SCP 75).

Once a Christian worker's family lost everything they had in a fire, including their automobiles. After the insurance settled, they needed nearly $20,000 just to replace what they needed to meet their basic needs. When this need was made known to our church family and other Christian friends, we were able to raise sufficient money to replace what they had lost. In so doing, those of us who "had plenty" at that time were able to help this family who was facing a crisis.

6. Working to Give

Stealing was a prominent activity in the Roman Empire. It was a particular temptation for slaves whose masters had become Christians. We have already seen this illustrated when Onesimus stole from his master Philemon. But stealing was a prevalent practice among all Romans, and it was not uncommon for these bad habits to carry over into the lives of those who professed Christ. As in other areas of morality and ethics, it took time for these people to know what God expected of them and then to respond obediently to the will of God. Consequently, Paul wrote, "He who has been stealing must steal no longer" (Ephesians 4:28*a*).

When giving this exhortation not to steal, however, Paul did not stop with a "thou shalt not." He went on to instruct these Christians to work harder so that they would have money left over to share with other people. He exhorted each of them to do "something useful with his own hands, that he may have something to share with those in need" (Ephesians 4:28*b*).

What an incredible testimony it must have been to see people reverse their field so dramatically. Rather than continuing to be *self-centered takers*, they actually became *Christlike givers.*

How many Christians in today's world begin the day on the job with the objective in mind to work hard in order to make money to give away? If this were our attitude, our "work" would definitely take on new meaning. Furthermore, our employers would be overwhelmed with our productivity. Think also of the doors this would open for a direct Christian witness. This is no doubt one of the things Peter had in mind when he wrote, "Live such good lives among the pagans that, though they accuse you of doing wrong, they may see your good deeds and glorify God on the day he visits us" (1 Peter 2:12).

It is no secret that many people do everything they can to get something for nothing. If they do not steal money outright from their employers, they steal time, which is a form of money. Paul stated that *Christians should never steal in any form or fashion; rather, we should be engaged in useful work, not only to take care of our own needs but to help meet the needs of others* (SCP 103).

7. Organizing to Meet Needs

Though the church in Jerusalem was unique in its structure, what they did to help widows illustrates another principle. When there are needs among Christians that are authentic and cannot be met in other ways, those needs should be met by members of the Body of Christ. However, this should be done in an orderly and systematic way. Consequently, *any given church in any given cultural situation should develop a proper system to determine what the needs of others are and then determine how to meet those needs in an equitable fashion* (SCP 12).

Applying this principle is sometimes difficult in a church that is growing rapidly. As in Jerusalem, the larger the church becomes, the easier it is to neglect people. Conversely, large numbers also add to the probability that some will attempt to take financial advantage of the church. Paul addressed these issues in his later letters (e.g., 2 Thessalonians 3:6-10). In his first letter to Timothy, he outlined some pointed requirements for being qualified to receive consistent help from the church (1 Timothy 5:3-16; see SCP 115). Translated into supracultural principles, these requirements are as follows:

• People in need of consistent help should look first to their own family and relatives.
• Spiritual leaders should make sure that all sources of help outside the church are explored before giving consistent financial assistance.
• Those receiving consistent help from the church should be older, mature believers (a widow in New Testament days had to be over sixty) who have demonstrated their maturity by having been morally pure, by developing respect from their own children and grandchildren, by being given to hospitality, and by having served others in the church.

8. Delegating Responsibility

It is not God's will that those responsible for teaching the Word of God be burdened with the responsibility of administering programs that meet the material needs of people (SCP 13). This principle was clearly illustrated in the Jerusalem church. The apostles were to make sure that the widows' needs were met. But they were to do so by setting up a proper system. They were not responsible for the actual distribution of food.

The reason for this principle is obvious. Since there are just so many hours in a day, God does not want those designated primarily as pastors and teachers in the local church to be sidetracked from fulfilling their primary ministry. Though social work is important, it should be done by other qualified leaders. That is why the apostles made clear that they could not "neglect the ministry of the Word of God" to personally care for the widows (Acts 6:2).

The apostle Paul reinforced this principle when he wrote to Timothy. First, he outlined the qualifications for elders (1 Timothy 3:1-7)—those who are responsible to shepherd and teach God's people. Then, he outlined the qualifications for deacons (1 Timothy 3:8-13)—men and women who are to serve in various roles in the church to meet physical needs. However, both elders and deacons who minister in these two areas are to be highly qualified people—which leads to our next principle.

9. SELECTING QUALIFIED PEOPLE

The Scriptures teach that *meeting the "spiritual needs" of people and meeting the "material needs" of people require the same basic standards when selecting leaders to meet those needs* (SCP 14). For example, the seven men who were appointed by the apostles to oversee the responsibility of meeting the needs of widows were to be "full of the Spirit and wisdom" (Acts 6:3). Furthermore, the men and women who were to occupy serving roles in the church in Ephesus were to also be highly qualified individuals (1 Timothy 3:8-13). Paul repeated many of the same basic qualifications for them as he did for those who were to serve as elders, or pastors and teachers (1 Timothy 3:1-7; Titus 1:6-9).

This indicates the value that God places on this area of ministry. Meeting spiritual needs and meeting material needs are both important areas in doing the will of God. They should not be separate in terms of importance but, rather, in terms of how to make sure both are done properly.

10. SETTING UP SPECIAL WELFARE SYSTEMS

When first-century Jews acknowledged Jesus Christ as their Messiah, they were deprived of financial aid from the third-tithe resources set aside by the priests. That is why the Grecian widows needed special help when the church was born in Jerusalem. That is also why the Christians in Antioch sent gifts of money to the Christians in Judea during a time of famine (Acts 11:19-30).

In the Western world particularly, welfare systems are set up within the governmental systems to help everyone. Christians benefit since they are part of the system. Consequently, local churches are not faced with the same degree of responsibility as were believers in the first-century world. Nevertheless, what is true in America and other free societies today does not exist in all parts of the world. Consequently, the principle that *Christians are responsible to set up welfare systems to take care of valid human needs* (SCP 51), applies directly in some cultures today just as it did in New Testament days.

11. BEING GIVEN TO HOSPITALITY

When the church was founded in Jerusalem, Christians had to find new places to be taught the Word of God and to worship. Though they initially gathered in the Temple courts, they were not long welcomed there. Consequently, they began to meet in homes all over the city.

When the Jerusalem believers were scattered and local congregations were planted in other places, neither could they meet in the numerous Jewish synagogues that graced the landscape in various cities throughout the

Roman Empire. Consequently, they continued to meet in homes and followed this practice for decades, until they were able to build church buildings sometime in the third century. Since the church was growing rapidly, only the more affluent Christians were able to provide homes large enough to house many of these growing churches.

One of the first recorded examples of this involves John Mark's mother. After Peter was miraculously released from prison in Jerusalem, "he went to the house of Mary the mother of John, also called Mark, where many people had gathered and were praying [she obviously had a large home]" (Acts 12:12). He "knocked at the outer entrance" and "a servant girl named Rhoda [only well-to-do people had outer entrances and servants] came to answer the door" (Acts 12:13). Mary was obviously a wealthy Jewish Christian lady who had opened her home to the believers in Jerusalem. We will see that this became a common practice among more affluent Christians as the church spread throughout the empire.

God desires that this principle be applied today in all parts of the world, not only among those who have an abundance of this world's goods. That does not mean we should not build church buildings, but it does mean that *God wants to use people who can use their homes in a special way to offer hospitality to other Christians* (SCP 46). In some instances, these homes may be small and "humble." But they should be used for God nevertheless.

12. WITHHOLDING ASSISTANCE FROM IRRESPONSIBLE CHRISTIANS

When Paul wrote to the Thessalonians, he gave a guideline that provides balance to everything we have learned thus far regarding meeting human needs. Out of context it would appear to be a harsh and insensitive exhortation: "If a man will not work, he shall not eat" (2 Thessalonians 3:10*b*).

In context the Thessalonians were not responding whatsoever to Paul's gracious and repetitious exhortations. Furthermore, Paul's intention was not to make these people suffer. Rather, he was attempting to "get their attention" to bring needed changes in their lives. Thus, Paul concluded by saying, "Do not associate with him [that is, any brother or sister who is idle] *in order that he [or she] may feel ashamed*" (2 Thessalonians 3:14).

To make sure that the Thessalonian Christians really understood his motives, Paul clarified that they should not regard this person "as an enemy," but "as a brother" (2 Thessalonians 3:15). In other words, they were to approach this individual as a member of the family of God, dealing with each person lovingly but firmly.

In essence, Paul was telling believers of all time that *Christians who can work for a living, but who do not, should not be given economic assistance* (SCP 66). He graphically illustrated in his letter, however, that this principle is to be practiced only after Christians have been thoroughly taught that they are out of the will of God and after they have persistently refused to respond. This principle is important to apply because lazy Christians who are given economic assistance will continue to take advantage of others' generosity. That is affirmed again and again in culture generally. People think of all kinds of ways to misuse and abuse welfare systems. Unfortunately, Christians are not exempt from this kind of behavior.

Probably no biblical principle is more difficult to apply in our culture today. Manipulative Christians can easily make other Christians feel guilty. It is difficult to resist a person who cries out, "How can you do this to me and call yourself a Christian?" However, a hungry stomach will do wonders for lazy Christians. As in other aspects of Christian living, where believers are not practicing the will of God, it sometimes takes a traumatic experience to enable these people to break out of their sinful habits.

This principle is also difficult to apply when more than one person is involved. Paul was certainly not teaching that we should be insensitive to innocent family members who become victims because of a lazy father or mother. Here again we must develop an approach that will discipline the offender without making innocent people suffer.

13. Sharing Personal Needs Discreetly

The Scriptures teach that *Christians should be open and honest about their material needs but that they should avoid any form of dishonesty and manipulation by playing on others' sympathy* (SCP 109). Paul illustrates this principle with his own life. He seldom talked about his own needs, but when he had one, he admitted it. Thus when he wrote to the Philippians, he said, "I rejoice greatly in the Lord that at last you have renewed your concern for me. Indeed, you have been concerned, but you had no opportunity to show it. I am not saying this because I am in need, for I have learned to be content whatever the circumstances" (Philippians 4:10-11).

Here Paul was letting the Philippians know how happy he was about the gift they had sent. However, he hurried to tell them that he was not playing on their sympathy. He was totally honest. He was always concerned that his motives never be misinterpreted. On some occasions, he actually refused what was coming to him as an apostle of Christ to avoid being a stumbling block to non-Christians or to new babes in Christ (1 Corinthians 9:1-18; 1 Thessalonians 2:9).

Unfortunately, some Christians today methodically work at giving the impression that they are always in need. Christian leaders who make their living doing religious work can also be tempted to take advantage of members of Christ's Body. This should never be. Unfortunately, there are some who do, which makes it very difficult for those who do not.

Paul is a marvelous example of sharing his needs openly but discreetly. May God give us more Christians with this kind of integrity.

14. ENTERTAINING THOSE WE DO NOT KNOW PERSONALLY

We have already looked at the directive in this chapter to "show hospitality" to fellow believers. But in Hebrews, Christians are encouraged "to show hospitality to *strangers*" (13:2*a*)—that is, to believers we do not know personally. To understand more clearly what the author of this letter had in mind, we need to look at the context.

He reminded his readers that "some people had entertained angels without knowing it" (Hebrews 13:2*b*). Most Bible commentators agree that the term "angels" in this instance refers to "messengers" who served Jesus Christ as apostles, prophets, evangelists, and pastors and teachers. These were "angel/messengers" who were assigned to these missionary responsibilities by Jesus Christ to equip and build up the universal Body of Christ (Ephesians 4:11-13). In other words, among the strangers who knocked on the doors of Christian dwellings were true servants of God who were called in a special way to carry out the Great Commission.

In applying this Scripture in our own cultural situation, we must understand that the Scriptures are not teaching us to have an "open door" and an "open hands" policy for every stranger who passes by and claims to be a Christian leader. The Scriptures do teach, however, that our generosity must extend beyond our own local churches. Though we may never be able to fellowship together face-to-face, all believers belong to the family of God.

Some people will take advantage of this principle of Christian hospitality. They know Christians are to be generous—even toward strangers—and they will purposely use this as a means to play on people's sympathy and their desire to do the will of God in all things.

As a pastor, I have had to deal with this problem over the years from those who claim to be Christians or Christian leaders in need. Since I tend to be vulnerable in this area, I have had to develop a strategy to handle these situations wisely. For example, I have asked for references I can call immediately for verification. This usually determines a true need, since fraudulent people will not give references, which, of course, disqualifies them for economic assistance.

A word of warning. Some people have learned to circumvent strategies. One woman called our church office for help since she and her children were about to be evicted from their apartment. We asked for her landlord's name and number. She gladly gave it, and we called for verification of her story. Sure enough, the landlord confirmed the eviction notice. However, we discovered later that the so-called "landlord" was probably involved in the scheme and had developed this subtle strategy to take advantage of our church financially.

We must be on guard, however, not to allow these experiences to cause us to be cynical, insensitive, and uncaring. The important point to remember from this passage in Hebrews is that *all Christians are to show hospitality, not only to those believers in a specific local Christian community but to those they may not know personally* (SCP 121).

Let's Check Ourselves

On a scale of one to ten, circle the number that best represents how well you believe the people in your church or group practice the biblical principle found in each question.

1. Do Christians in our church make unusual sacrifices to meet special material needs, particularly as they exist in our own local fellowship?

VERY LITTLE   SOMEWHAT   EXTENSIVELY
1   2   3   4   5   6   7   8   9   10

2. Are people in our church motivated to give because of consistent human needs, especially within our local body?

VERY LITTLE   SOMEWHAT   EXTENSIVELY
1   2   3   4   5   6   7   8   9   10

3. Do the grown children in our church take proper care of their parents if they have special material needs?

VERY LITTLE   SOMEWHAT   EXTENSIVELY
1   2   3   4   5   6   7   8   9   10

4. Do the people in our church understand the special place God has in His heart for those who have serious physical needs and for those who help meet these needs?

VERY LITTLE   SOMEWHAT   EXTENSIVELY
1   2   3   4   5   6   7   8   9   10

5. Do people in our church who have an abundance realize that they should be willing to share some of their excess with other Christians in crisis, who are unable to care for their physical needs at that particular time?

VERY LITTLE   SOMEWHAT   EXTENSIVELY
1   2   3   4   5   6   7   8   9   10

6. Do the people in our church consider their vocational tasks an opportunity not only to make an honest living but to accumulate money to give to God's work?

VERY LITTLE				SOMEWHAT				EXTENSIVELY	
1	2	3	4	5	6	7	8	9	10

7. Do we have an efficient and effective system for meeting the material needs of those in our church who are hurting financially?

VERY LITTLE				SOMEWHAT				EXTENSIVELY	
1	2	3	4	5	6	7	8	9	10

8. Do the spiritual leaders in our church (pastors, elders, etc.) look to other qualified people to help meet the material needs of others?

VERY LITTLE				SOMEWHAT				EXTENSIVELY	
1	2	3	4	5	6	7	8	9	10

9. Do we require biblical qualifications for those who not only lead the church spiritually but for those who are selected to care for the material needs of people?

VERY LITTLE				SOMEWHAT				EXTENSIVELY	
1	2	3	4	5	6	7	8	9	10

10. Does our church help believers outside, as well as inside, our own local fellowship who are in physical need but who do not have access to sufficient resources to meet their needs?

VERY LITTLE				SOMEWHAT				EXTENSIVELY	
1	2	3	4	5	6	7	8	9	10

11. Are the people in our church demonstrating hospitality to both Christians and non-Christians by using their homes to entertain, conduct Bible studies, and host other small group meetings?

VERY LITTLE				SOMEWHAT				EXTENSIVELY	
1	2	3	4	5	6	7	8	9	10

12. Are the people in our church cautious about financially helping people who may be taking advantage, and are they, at the same time, applying principles of love and caring for those who are truly in need?

VERY LITTLE				SOMEWHAT				EXTENSIVELY	
1	2	3	4	5	6	7	8	9	10

13. Are the people in our church able to discern when Christian leaders on television and radio, and even in some churches, are using manipulative and dishonest tactics to get people to give?

VERY LITTLE				SOMEWHAT				EXTENSIVELY	
1	2	3	4	5	6	7	8	9	10

14. Do Christians in our church make an effort to show hospitality to reputable believers they may know only by name and not personally?

VERY LITTLE				SOMEWHAT				EXTENSIVELY	
1	2	3	4	5	6	7	8	9	10

How to Use This Evaluation Exercise

1. Duplicate these fourteen questions on a separate sheet, and have each person in your group anonymously evaluate your church.
2. Tabulate the responses to find an average score. To do so, total the numbers circled in each question. Divide this total number by the number of people responding to that particular question. This will give you a "mean," or average, score.
3. Discover the greatest needs in your church by arranging the scores numerically from the highest to the lowest. Those scores that are lowest represent the areas that need immediate attention.
4. In discussing these scores and the principles involved, spend time first of all reviewing the areas of strength in your church. Spend time in prayer, thanking God for those strengths.
5. Finally, spend time discussing ways to practice the principles that are the most neglected in your church. The following questions will help:
   a. What are the areas of greatest need?
   b. What can we do that we are not doing to practice these biblical principles?
   c. What specific goals can we set up to practice these principles?
   d. What can we do *immediately*?

Personalize This Project

Follow the procedure described at the end of chapter 1.

6

Giving with Proper Motives

Christians must give to be in God's will. However, to please God, Christians must also give with proper motives. How can we obey God in both respects? The Scriptures give us some definite guidelines to help us answer this question.

1. Giving in View of Christ's Return

The expectancy of the second coming of Jesus Christ should always be a strong motivational factor in the way Christians view and use their material possessions (SCP 18). This principle is illustrated throughout Scripture.

In the early days of the church, believers expected Christ to return rather quickly to set up His kingdom on earth. There is no question that this affected their desire to please the Lord with their earthly possessions. As we follow the biblical record, however, we discover that Christians became more tentative regarding the imminency of Christ's return. Predictably, this affected the way they related to their possessions. Understandably, they had to face the reality that they might live out their lives on earth before Christ returned and that they had to function as responsible citizens, caring for their material needs (2 Thessalonians 3:10). The next step was to begin to focus more and more on the security and status that comes from owning houses and lands and accumulating wealth. This tendency began to permeate Christianity soon after the first century—and has continued to this very day.

Those of us living in twentieth-century Western culture have probably been affected by materialism more significantly than any group of Christians since the time of Christ. It is easy to allow weeks and months, and even years, to go by without even thinking about the possible return of Jesus Christ. And when we do, we seldom contemplate our eternal rewards and what Christ would say should we suddenly stand before His judgment seat

67

to give an account of how we used our material possessions while on earth. Yet this should be a primary motivating factor regarding how we use our earthly possessions.

Paul pleaded for godly and righteous living "while we wait for the blessed hope—the glorious appearing of our great God and Savior, Jesus Christ" (Titus 2:13). Why this emphasis on holiness? Because Jesus Christ "gave himself for us to redeem us from all wickedness and to purify for himself a people that are his very own, *eager to do what is good*" (Titus 2:14).

A number of statements in Scripture encourage us to "do good" with the resources we have at our disposal. Part of that motivation for doing good while we have opportunity is that one day—perhaps soon—Jesus Christ will return and that opportunity will no longer exist.

2. Giving to Honor God and Not Ourselves

Glorifying God relates to everything a Christian does. Paul underscored this point when he wrote, "So whether you eat or drink or whatever you do, *do it all for the glory of God*" (1 Corinthians 10:31). This exhortation certainly includes the way we use our money and other material resources.

This spiritual guideline points to at least one major reason Luke recorded the story of Ananias and Sapphira immediately following Barnabas's generous act of love (Acts 4:34-36; 5:1-10). They, too, wanted to sell a piece of property that they owned and to give the proceeds to help others. However, their motive was entirely wrong. They wanted self-glory—so much so that they gave a false impression and actually lied to the Holy Spirit.

Ananias and Sapphira were not out of the will of God when they gave this money publicly. Many others throughout Jerusalem were doing the same thing. Neither was it wrong to keep back part of the money. There was no obligation either to sell the land or to give the money. Peter made that point clear. The sin that brought death was not even in giving a false impression to other believers—though certainly this was involved. The essence of the sin was in lying to God (Acts 5:3-4) and in testing the Holy Spirit (Acts 5:9).

What we see in the lives of Ananias and Sapphira is an ultimate demonstration of self-oriented giving. Stated as a positive principle, *what we give should always be given to honor God and not ourselves* (SCP 9).

3. Avoiding Hypocrisy and Dishonesty

Though serious punishment is not God's normal way of dealing with sin in the lives of His children, the Ananias and Sapphira story illustrates that *God detests dishonesty and lack of integrity when it comes to steward-ship* (Acts 5:1-10; SCP 10). Periodically in Scripture, God judged sins severely in the lives of His children. Ananias and Sapphira lost their lives. On another occasion, God severely judged some of the Corinthian Christians because they had so flagrantly abused the Lord's Supper (1 Corinthians 11:27). Paul explained that this was why many of these believers were "weak and sick" and a number of them had actually died (1 Corinthians 11:30).

On these rare occasions, God is reminding us how serious it is to violate His instructions and to purposely walk out of His will—especially when we know what His will is. It is only because of His grace and love that we are not always disciplined severely for our deliberate disobedience. Therefore, let us not ignore His love and abuse His grace. As Paul taught the Roman Christians, so let these words teach us: "Shall we go on sinning so that grace may increase? By no means! We died to sin; how can we live in it any longer?" (Romans 6:1-2). This injunction certainly includes the way we use our money and other resources.

4. CHECKING OUR MOTIVES

To avoid the sin committed by Ananias and Sapphira, *we should periodically check our motives to see if we are giving to glorify God or to glorify ourselves* (SCP 24). Jesus underscored the importance of correct motives when He taught, "when you give to the needy, do not let your left hand know what your right hand is doing, so that your giving may be in secret" (Matthew 6:3-4).

Some people have interpreted this teaching to mean that no one should ever know what a Christian gives. If this were true, however, none of us would even be able to know what we ourselves are giving. Furthermore, to be consistent, we would never be able to pray in public since Jesus in the very same context said, "When you pray go into your room, close the door, and pray to your Father, who is unseen" (Matthew 6:6*a*).

Looking at what Jesus actually practiced and promoted will help us understand what Jesus was saying. Generally speaking, He never condemned people who gave publicly. In fact, as the poor widow put her gift into the Temple treasury, He used her public offering to illustrate sacrificial giving to those who were watching (Luke 21:1-4).

Jesus was directing His exhortation primarily at the religious leaders for giving with false motives. When they gave to the needy, they would "announce it with trumpets" (Matthew 6:2*a*). Their motivation was solely "to be honored by men" (Matthew 6:2*b*). By teaching that giving should be a private matter, Jesus was removing their wrong motivation. If they could not be seen by men, they would have felt no need whatsoever to give—or to pray.

In essence, Jesus was teaching that, as Christians, we should periodically check our motives to see if we are giving to glorify God or to glorify ourselves. We need to ask ourselves several questions: What if no one knew what we were giving? Would we give to the same degree? On the other hand, what if others did know what we were giving? Would we be embarrassed and ashamed?

Christians can go to two extremes in this matter. For example, a "doctrine of public giving" per se can lead to self-glorification. Conversely, a "doctrine of private giving" per se can lead to another form of sin—"self-orientation." We are particularly vulnerable to this kind of sin when we are not being held accountable to be good stewards of what God has given us. In short, we may be using our "doctrine of privacy" to cover up our disobedience.

It is possible to blend and balance these basic factors in our giving. Our motive for public giving should be to honor God. Once we understand God's perspective on this issue and once we are giving as God intended us to give, we will not be concerned that our giving be kept confidential. In fact, we will feel good (not proud) that we are obeying God and modeling God's will to others. Once we have a biblical point of view on the way God wants us to use our material possessions, we will not want to keep this aspect of our Christian lives private any more than we want to keep private our commitment to moral and ethical behavior.

5. EVALUATING OUR THOUGHTS

Jesus taught that where our treasure is, there our heart will also be (Matthew 6:21). Here Jesus was teaching us that *we can test our focus regarding material possessions by what occupies our attitudes and actions* (SCP 27). If we are constantly concerned about our possessions on earth—thinking about them, worrying about them, demonstrating jealousy and greed, mistreating others to gain more or to keep what we have—our treasures are on earth. That is where our heart is. Conversely, if we are consistently thinking in terms of how we can use our material possessions to glorify God—how we can meet others' needs, how we can further God's work, how we can invest in eternal purposes—then our treasure is in heaven because that is where our heart is.

The following questions will help each of us determine our true perspective toward material possessions:

• What do I think about the most?

• What occupies most of my emotional and physical energy?

• How do I respond emotionally when I see human needs?

• How do I respond emotionally when I hear biblical messages on what God says my attitudes and actions should be regarding material possessions?

• How do I respond when I feel I may need to part with some material possessions that could better be used to meet someone else's needs or to help carry out the Great Commission?

- What priorities do I have other than making money (such as worshiping God, learning the Word of God, spending quality time with my family, serving others in my church, bettering the community)?
- What is my attitude in general toward giving?

6. GIVING GENEROUSLY BUT VOLUNTARILY

God wants all His children to be generous. However, *what Christians give should always be voluntary and from a heart of love and concern* (SCP 11). Peter made this point clear when he addressed Ananias. Referring to both his property and the money that he had received from the sale, Peter asked, "Didn't it belong to you before it was sold? And after it was sold, wasn't the money at your disposal?" (Acts 5:4).

God wants our gifts. If we do not give generously in relationship to our resources, we are out of His will. Conversely, God wants our gifts to come from generous hearts that respond apart from coercion. Paul affirmed this principle in the context of some of his strongest exhortations to be generous: "Each man should give . . . *not reluctantly or under compulsion*, for God loves a cheerful giver" (2 Corinthians 9:7).

7. GIVING FROM THE HEART

Paul also made clear that *every Christian is ultimately responsible to give to God on the basis of his or her own heart decision*: "Each man should give what he has decided in his heart to give" (2 Corinthians 9:7a; SCP 82).

Does this mean that Christians should not give if they cannot give from a cheerful heart? If this were true, Paul would not have encouraged the Corinthians to give when they had negative attitudes. His hope, of course, was that careful planning would refocus their motives.

That is the primary point Paul was making in the total context of this passage. We must give careful attention to planning our giving. We must be prepared when opportunities come our way. Lack of preparation and organization will always lead to resentment and resistance. Therefore, all of us are responsible to make sure we order our lives accordingly—which, in turn, will lead to joy and blessings in giving.

This principle applies to everything we do as Christians. If we waited until we felt like being obedient to every aspect of God's will, we would be consistently disobedient. Many aspects of love are difficult to apply—such as being patient and kind and unselfish (1 Corinthians 13:4-6). Positive feelings often follow right actions. So it is in giving. However, when all is said and done, God wants us to respond joyfully and cheerfully—which will happen if we attempt to apply these principles consistently.

8. Giving in Response to God's Grace

When Paul exhorted the Corinthians to give regularly and systematically, he reminded them that he was not *commanding* them. Rather, he wanted to "test the sincerity" of their love "by comparing it with the earnestness of others" (2 Corinthians 8:8). He then followed this exhortation with the example of Jesus Christ: "For you know the grace of our Lord Jesus Christ, that though he was rich, yet for your sakes he became poor, so that you through his poverty might become rich" (2 Corinthians 8:9).

Paul was reminding the Corinthians that Jesus demonstrated the greatest act of grace ever performed. In essence, the apostle was communicating to these New Testament Christians (and to us) that when we truly understand what Christ has done for each of us, a "command" should not be necessary in terms of our response to God's love. By implication, Paul was also teaching us that when we do not give regularly, systematically, proportionately, and joyfully, we do not have a proper perspective on our Savior's incarnation. Neither do we have a proper appreciation of "God's mercies" in providing for our redemption. When we have this total perspective, what appears to be a moral duty and responsibility becomes a wonderful and joyous privilege (see SCP 73).

9. Testing Our Faith

"Faith by itself, if it is not accompanied by action, is dead" (James 2:17). Viewed in isolation, this statement appears to be quite general. However, in context, James was writing about how Christians use their material resources. Since there are many ways we can reflect our faith, it is significant that James chose this aspect of our lives to illustrate good works. To focus the problem James asked two questions: "What good is it, my brothers, if a man claims to have faith but has no deeds? Can such faith save him?" (2:14)

To make his point, James used the same technique he employed earlier in this chapter (2:2). He posed a hypothetical situation that was probably based on reality. "Suppose," James wrote, "a brother or sister is without clothes and daily food. If one of you says to him, 'Go, I wish you well; keep warm and well fed,' but does nothing about his physical needs, what good is it? In the same way," James concluded, "faith by itself, if it is not accompanied by action, is dead" (James 2:15-17).

When evaluating whether or not a person's relationship with Jesus Christ is truly authentic, we seldom, if ever, answer this question based upon how a person uses his material possessions. On the other hand, Christian leaders frequently refer to a person's morality or ethics to test faith. Why not use a person's materialistic and selfish behavior? This is an appropriate question, since *the way we use our material possessions is the very illustration James uses to test whether or not we are truly saved* (SCP 57).

Obviously, we must be cautious in applying this principle lest we be guilty of judging another Christian. The safest approach is to "judge ourselves" so that we do not "come under judgment" (1 Corinthians 11:31).

LET'S CHECK OURSELVES

On a scale of one to ten, circle the number that best represents how well you believe the people in your church or group practice the biblical principle found in each question.

1. Are the people in our church motivated to give because of the truth that Jesus Christ could come at any moment and require an accounting of how we have used our material possessions?

VERY LITTLE				SOMEWHAT				EXTENSIVELY	
1	2	3	4	5	6	7	8	9	10

2. Do the people in our church give to honor God and not themselves?

VERY LITTLE				SOMEWHAT				EXTENSIVELY	
1	2	3	4	5	6	7	8	9	10

3. Is the giving in our church free from dishonesty, lack of integrity, and hypocrisy?

VERY LITTLE				SOMEWHAT				EXTENSIVELY	
1	2	3	4	5	6	7	8	9	10

4. Do we encourage people in our church to periodically evaluate their motives for giving?

VERY LITTLE				SOMEWHAT				EXTENSIVELY	
1	2	3	4	5	6	7	8	9	10

5. Do the people in our church focus their attention on their material possessions rather than on doing God's will in every respect?

VERY LITTLE				SOMEWHAT				EXTENSIVELY	
1	2	3	4	5	6	7	8	9	10

6. Is the giving in our church motivated by concern for God and others and a desire to see God's purposes fulfilled in the world?

VERY LITTLE				SOMEWHAT				EXTENSIVELY	
1	2	3	4	5	6	7	8	9	10

7. Are the Christians in our church making decisions to give based upon internal motivation rather than simply from a sense of obligation?

VERY LITTLE				SOMEWHAT				EXTENSIVELY	
1	2	3	4	5	6	7	8	9	10

8. Are believers in our church giving to God's work primarily out of gratitude to God for His grace rather than from a sense of obligation?

VERY LITTLE				SOMEWHAT				EXTENSIVELY	
1	2	3	4	5	6	7	8	9	10

9. Am I reflecting the reality of my conversion to Christ by being a generous, unselfish Christian?

VERY LITTLE				SOMEWHAT				EXTENSIVELY	
1	2	3	4	5	6	7	8	9	10

How to Use This Evaluation Exercise

1. Duplicate these nine questions on a separate sheet, and have each person in your group anonymously evaluate your church.
2. Tabulate the responses to find an average score. To do so, total the numbers circled in each question. Divide this total number by the number of people responding to that particular question. This will give you a "mean," or average, score.
3. Discover the greatest needs in your church by arranging the scores numerically from the highest to the lowest. Those scores that are lowest represent the areas that need immediate attention.
4. In discussing these scores and the principles involved, spend time first of all reviewing the areas of strength in your church. Spend time in prayer, thanking God for those strengths.
5. Finally, spend time discussing ways to practice the principles that are the most neglected in your church. The following questions will help:
   a. What are the areas of greatest need?
   b. What can we do that we are not doing to practice these biblical principles?
   c. What specific goals can we set up to practice these principles?
   d. What can we do *immediately*?

Personalize This Project

Follow the procedure described at the end of chapter 1.

7

Leadership Responsibility and Accountability

When all is said and done, the final responsibility for helping Christians obey God with their material possessions falls on the shoulders of spiritual leaders. Paul, particularly, demonstrates and illustrates with his own life, and in the letters he wrote to the churches, God's will in this matter. A number of scriptural principles can enable all Christian leaders to be responsible and accountable both to God and to those they lead and serve. These principles can also motivate believers to respond biblically to their leaders as they attempt to apply these truths.

1. FOCUSING ON THE LOCAL CHURCH

The church began in Jerusalem. From there it spread around the world. Great sections of the New Testament involve letters written to local churches (localized expressions of the universal church) or to individuals (such as Timothy and Titus) who were involved in local church ministry.

Any view, then, *of how Christians should use their material possessions must focus first and foremost on local churches* (SCP 16, 87). Christian leaders have the responsibility to teach and practice this principle. To bypass this important concept in Scripture is, in essence, to ignore what is recorded by gifted men inspired by the Holy Spirit. Furthermore, as will be demonstrated in future chapters, if Christians bypass the concept of the local church in their giving, they will inevitably violate a number of important biblical principles.

Do not misunderstand. The fact that God allows "freedom in form" for the church has given birth to many legitimate ministries we call parachurch organizations. In many instances, these organizations perform the same functions as God intended for local churches, both in the areas of evangelism and edification. However, before we support any particular parachurch ministry financially, it is important to view that ministry through the lens of biblical ecclesiology. In other words, we must carefully evaluate the functions and goals of every parachurch ministry by what Scripture teaches about God's will for the local church.

- How does a particular parachurch's ministry philosophy square with what God says about the local church?
- How does that respective ministry view the local church?
- Is that particular ministry working in harmony with the concept of the local church or does its approach virtually ignore the local church?

The answers to these questions will provide biblical guidelines to help determine whether or not to support a given parachurch ministry.

2. Being Trustworthy

As the church grew and expanded throughout the New Testament world, so did the number of people who wanted to get into leadership roles in the church out of purely selfish motives. Though an age-old problem (as we have seen with Simon the sorcerer in Samaria), more and more people wanted to "cash in" on this unique opportunity. Because of their very commitment and character, Christians were vulnerable to being led astray by self-serving leaders.

With this in mind, Paul wrote to Timothy and made clear that *Christians who occupy leadership roles in the church should be completely trustworthy when it came to financial matters* (SCP 114). An elder was not to be "a lover of money." The same was true of deacons. They were to be men and women who would never pursue "dishonest gain" (1 Timothy 3:2-3, 8). The apostle Peter showed the same concern. Do not be "greedy for money," he wrote to elders, but be "eager to serve" (1 Peter 5:2).

The same principle applies today—and even more so. With the advent of modern media (print, radio, television, video), Christian hucksters have come "out of the woodwork." They are experts in taking advantage of naive and caring Christians. And one of their points of strategy is what has come to be called "prosperity theology." Not only do they appeal to our God-given desire to obey God, they blend this desire with our natural tendency to want to be blessed materially. Consequently, they have developed a "self-centered" approach to giving that has become an incredible heresy in the twentieth-century world. Unfortunately, it has worked among many of God's people and, in the process, has padded the pockets of a number of "so-called" spiritual leaders.

This is another reason Christians ought to focus their giving in their local churches, where spiritual leaders can be approved and appointed by those who know their true character. These spiritual leaders can more easily be held accountable, although operating at a local church level in itself is not a guarantee against dishonesty and greed. However, this kind of inappropriate behavior is less likely to occur if a local church is functioning according to the biblical principles that are so clearly outlined in the Word of God.[1]

3. Being Accountable

Those who handle and distribute monies given to God's work should not only be above reproach in all respects but should also be held accountable (SCP 69). Therefore, Paul wrote to the Corinthians: "Then, when I arrive, I will give letters of introduction to the men *you approve* and send them with your gift to Jerusalem. If it seems advisable for me to go also, they will accompany me" (1 Corinthians 16:3-4).

Though Paul planned this collection, he did not handle the money personally. He exhorted the Corinthians to raise the funds, to store it up, and to keep it until he arrived, and then they were to choose people they personally trusted to transport the gift. True to form, Paul wanted to be above reproach in all respects so that no one could accuse him of raising this money to benefit himself.

Paul was also extremely cautious as to how and when he received monies to meet his own personal needs. He did not want to give anyone an opportunity to question his motives or to accuse him of misappropriating or misusing funds. That is an important principle in a world where some prominent Christian leaders have been guilty of violating God's will in this matter. To follow Paul's model, the Christian leader should

- Set up an accountability plan whereby he does not have to handle money personally.
- Set up a careful reporting and accountability system.
- Never make decisions on his own regarding the amounts of money he personally receives.
- Make sure that more than one person handles the money.
- Make sure people who handle money are approved by others who know them to be men and women of integrity.

4. Teaching Stewardship Responsibility

Ultimately, God will hold spiritual leaders accountable for the way *they have taught believers what He says about material possessions* (SCP 38). Christian leaders need to relate specific examples of how to apply these principles, as well as teach the principles themselves. In doing so they follow the example of Jesus. James, in his relatively brief letter, included eight major teachings about material possessions and illustrated these truths specifically and dramatically. The apostle Paul included at least sixteen major teachings on giving in the space of two chapters (2 Corinthians 8-9).

5. SHARING EMOTIONAL RISKS

Handling money in God's work is a heavy responsibility. One reason for this is the emotional risks involved. There will be rejection and criticism from those who are either carnal or selfish. There will be criticism even from those who simply do not understand—or who do not want to understand. And there will always be potential accusations of dishonesty or selfishness from both Christians and non-Christians.

Paul faced all these painful problems, even though his motives were always pure. He faced emotional reactions from Christians simply because he was teaching an aspect of the will of God that always makes people feel guilty and uncomfortable when they are, at that moment, living outside the will of God.

Every Christian leader who is faithful in trying to care for economic needs while doing God's work and who, at the same time, teaches what God has to say about faithful stewardship will face the same problems. *No Christian leader should have to bear this burden alone* (SCP 76). Like Paul, we need to share this responsibility with others (2 Corinthians 8:16-17, 23).

The importance of this principle has impacted my own life as a pastor. Our church, along with many churches in the Dallas area, was affected by the oil and real estate crisis. Many people in our churches who were doing well economically were suddenly faced with unusual financial pressures. Some were overwhelmed with indebtedness, and it took everything they were making just to maintain their previous life-style. Since many of these people had not been giving out of their "firstfruits" but out of what was left over, God's work suffered.

This crisis put pressure on all the spiritual leaders of the church. As the senior pastor, giving direction to a large staff, I felt a deep sense of responsibility to my fellow pastors who had families to care for and bills to meet. Frankly, I "worried" about being able to pay their salaries.

A man in our church sensed the pressure on me and offered to help in any way to carry the burden. To make a long story short, which I describe in my book *A Biblical Theology of Material Possessions*, the elders appointed a special task force we called the "Acts 6 Group." They joined hands with me and with the elders to bear this financial burden. In fact, this book, as well as the full-length theological work, grew out of this process.

The first thing we did was to study together what the Bible actually says about material possessions. In turn, these men helped me prepare a series of biblical messages on this subject. When I delivered these messages, communicating what the Bible says about how Christians should view and use their material possessions, they stood firmly with me. What a blessing to share this emotional burden with a group of godly men. I am indeed grateful. I am thankful for Paul's model in this regard.

6. Maintaining a High Level of Communication

Christian leaders who always maintain a high level of communication enable believers to be obedient to God's will in the way they use their material possessions (SCP 88). Paul certainly illustrated this principle, particularly in his communication with the Thessalonians and Corinthians.

First, note Paul's extensive communication with the Thessalonians:

He modeled stewardship principles with his own life (Acts 18:3; 2 Thessalonians 3:7-9).

He taught these believers their stewardship responsibility face-to-face after he led them to Christ (2 Thessalonians 3:10).

He wrote them a letter and reminded them of the way he and his missionary companions had modeled stewardship principles (1 Thessalonians 2:7-9).

He taught them a second time in his letter that they should be responsible in this area of their lives (1 Thessalonians 4:11-12).

He ended his first letter by exhorting all believers in Thessalonica to admonish those who were not diligent (1 Thessalonians 4:14).

Note the same level of communication when he dealt with the Corinthians:

He gave them definite instructions as he closed his first letter (1 Corinthians 16:2).

He followed up these instructions by sending Titus to meet with them personally to reinforce what he had written (2 Corinthians 8:6).

He wrote a second letter, responding to their questions and reactions by sharing with them the Macedonian model (2 Corinthians 8:1-5).

He elaborated extensively as to why they should finish the project they had begun (2 Corinthians 8:7-15).

He also told them he was going to send Titus back again, accompanied by two additional men, to help them follow through (2 Corinthians 8:16-24; 9:5).

Paul sensitively reminded the Corinthians that it was they who had motivated the Macedonians to give in the first place (2 Corinthians 9:1-4).

To avoid any embarrassment, he informed the Corinthians that some of the Macedonians would probably be with him when they came to receive the gift they promised to give (2 Corinthians 9:4).

No one can question Paul's intense communication when it came to informing Christians regarding their financial responsibilities. To some, the steps he took may appear redundant, but the Holy Spirit knew that Christian leaders down through the centuries needed these examples of communication. He also knew that Christians need to understand why this kind of communication is essential.

God has ordained this process because He is aware, first of all, that most Christians find it easy to be negligent in doing the will of God in this area. Second, God also knows His children often do not hear what He says without extensive repetition. That is why He has given us a book that contains "many books"—both in the Old and New Testaments—filled with repetition.

7. Communicating Directly But Sensitively

The Scriptures clearly teach that *spiritual leaders should utilize methods of communication that create both a sense of obligation and a spirit of spontaneity and freedom in giving* (SCP 100). Paul demonstrated this unique balance on several occasions. In almost "tongue-in-cheek" fashion, he wrote to Philemon:

> But I did not want to do anything without your consent so that any favor you do will be *spontaneous and not forced.* . . . If he [Onesimus] has done you any wrong or owes you anything, charge it to me. I, Paul, am writing this with my own hand. I will pay it back—not to mention that *you owe me your very self.* (Philemon 14, 18-19)

Onesimus had wronged Philemon. He owed him the money or goods he had stolen. Consequently, Paul informed his friend that he would pay it back for Onesimus. But in the same breath, he reminded Philemon that he owed his very conversion to their previous interaction about the gospel of Christ.

Though this may look like manipulation, it was Paul's gentle but straightforward way of being honest. If Philemon felt any sense of guilt at this moment, Paul would not consider that to be his problem but Philemon's. He owed Paul a debt that he could never repay with his material possessions.

Paul demonstrated this unique balance on other occasions. He let the believers in Corinth know that he knew how eager they were to help the poor Christians in Jerusalem. In fact, he even told them that he did not feel it necessary to write to them about it. But just in case they did not understand, he wrote anyway. In addition, he sent "the brothers in order that" his boasting about them would not prove to be untrue. He wanted them to be ready with the gift so that he would not be embarrassed and neither would they (2 Corinthians 9:1-4).

All of us, then, need a certain amount of "God-designed pressure" in order to be faithful and obedient to God. True, we may feel a certain amount of guilt. However, when we are out of the will of God, we *should* feel guilt. If we do not, we may have already allowed our consciences to become hardened to the Word of God and to the Holy Spirit (1 Timothy 4:2).

8. SILENCING UNQUALIFIED LEADERS

Paul had very little patience with men and women who were teaching false doctrines and manipulating people in order to pursue dishonest gain. Writing to Titus, he said: "They must be silenced, because they are ruining whole households" (Titus 1:11; see SCP 118). This is a difficult principle to practice for several reasons.

First, we do not have the same revelatory insight and direct authority as Paul and certain other apostolic leaders.

Second, many leaders who are guilty of this kind of behavior today are outside of the accountability system of a local church or even of a denomination. This is particularly true of those who have developed a "ministry at large" by means of radio and television.

Third, some of our legal systems have become so complex that even our government finds it difficult to prosecute and silence these people.

There are some things we can do, however.

First, all churches should have a system of checks and balances that make it virtually impossible for a Christian leader to practice this kind of behavior.

Second, if lack of accountability occurs and if nothing is done to correct the situation, Christians should not continue to support that church with contributions or attendance.

Third, Christians should not support any Christian organization where its leaders are violating the basic principles outlined in Scripture regarding material possessions.

Fourth, Christian leaders who have the authority to do so should not avoid confronting and exposing people who are violating the principles of the Word of God.

Fifth, Christians should do all they can to support Christian leaders who are committed to practicing the principles of Scripture.

Sixth, Christians should pray that God will protect Christian leaders from falling into Satan's trap.

NOTE

1. See the first part of chapter 8 for further discussion of prosperity theology. Also see Michael Horton, ed., *The Agony of Deceit: What Some TV Preachers Are Really Teaching* (Chicago: Moody, 1990); Bruce Barron, *The Health and Wealth Gospel: A Fresh*

Look at Healing, Prosperity & Positive Confession (Downers Grove, Ill.: InterVarsity, 1987).

LET'S CHECK OURSELVES

On a scale of one to ten, circle the number that best represents how well you believe the people in your church or group practice the biblical principle found in each question.

1. Do the people in our church first and foremost support the ministry of our local fellowship?

VERY LITTLE   SOMEWHAT   EXTENSIVELY

1   2   3   4   5   6   7   8   9   10

2. Are our spiritual leaders selected on the basis of the biblical requirements that they not be "lovers of money" nor those who "pursue dishonest gain"?

VERY LITTLE   SOMEWHAT   EXTENSIVELY

1   2   3   4   5   6   7   8   9   10

3. Are those who handle the money in our church accountable and above reproach in every respect?

VERY LITTLE   SOMEWHAT   EXTENSIVELY

1   2   3   4   5   6   7   8   9   10

4. Do the spiritual leaders in our church regularly and consistently teach our people God's will regarding how to view and use their material possessions?

VERY LITTLE   SOMEWHAT   EXTENSIVELY

1   2   3   4   5   6   7   8   9   10

5. Do leaders other than our primary pastor help carry the burden for meeting the financial needs of our church?

VERY LITTLE   SOMEWHAT   EXTENSIVELY

1   2   3   4   5   6   7   8   9   10

6. Have the leaders in our church developed a communication methodology that enables them to communicate efficiently and continually, but sensitively, about our responsibility to share material possessions?

VERY LITTLE   SOMEWHAT   EXTENSIVELY

1   2   3   4   5   6   7   8   9   10

7. Do leaders in our church communicate in proper balance between giving out of obligation and giving spontaneously out of willing hearts?

VERY LITTLE SOMEWHAT EXTENSIVELY

1	2	3	4	5	6	7	8	9	10

8. Do the people in our church make an effort to silence false teachers by not supporting them financially?

VERY LITTLE SOMEWHAT EXTENSIVELY

1	2	3	4	5	6	7	8	9	10

How to Use This Evaluation Exercise

1. Duplicate these eight questions on a separate sheet, and have each person in your group anonymously evaluate your church.
2. Tabulate the responses to find an average score. To do so, total the numbers circled in each question. Divide this total number by the number of people responding to that particular question. This will give you a "mean," or average, score.
3. Discover the greatest needs in your church by arranging the scores numerically from the highest to the lowest. Those scores that are lowest represent the areas that need immediate attention.
4. In discussing these scores and the principles involved, spend time first of all reviewing the areas of strength in your church. Spend time in prayer, thanking God for those strengths.
5. Finally, spend time discussing ways to practice the principles that are the most neglected in your church. The following questions will help:
   a. What are the areas of greatest need?
   b. What can we do that we are not doing to practice these biblical principles?
   c. What specific goals can we set up to practice these principles?
   d. What can we do *immediately*?

Personalizing This Project

Since these questions are designed primarily for leaders, they can only be effectively personalized by pastors, elders, deacons, etc. Unless you occupy one of these positions, you will find it difficult to complete this exercise. If you are a leader, however, follow the same procedure as in preceding chapters.

8

God's Blessings for Faithful Giving

Widespread misunderstanding exists regarding God's blessings for faithful giving. Some believe that God's promises for faithful giving are primarily temporal. Others teach that these blessings are largely spiritual and eternal. A true biblical perspective involves both, but with a strong focus on our future life in heaven. God does promise to meet our needs on this earth, but His greatest blessings will be eternal.

1. DAILY PROVISIONS

One thing is clear in both the Old and New Testaments: *God desires to bless us and provide us with the necessities of life* (SCP 29). When Jesus taught His disciples to pray, He exhorted them to ask for their daily bread (Matthew 6:11). The apostle Paul later affirmed and broadened Jesus' specific exhortation: "Do not be anxious about *anything*, but in *everything* by prayer and petition, with thanksgiving, present your requests to God" (Philippians 4:6). In Jesus' model prayer, He gave "specificity" to the "everything" that Paul mentioned in his exhortation to the Philippians.

It is our privilege, then, to ask God for "daily bread." Though there are times when Christians suffer—along with all humanity—because of natural disasters and human frailty, God wants to encourage us, whether we have little or much. *We should never hesitate to ask Him to meet our needs* (SCP 25). Not to do so is to violate His will for our lives. Providing for our daily sustenance is one of God's present blessings for being faithful to Him.

In terms of our material needs, we should remember, however, that God in His sovereignty sometimes allows difficult economic situations to refocus our thinking from dependency on ourselves to dependency on Him. How easy it is during times of plenty to revert to Israel's behavior and say "We did this ourselves."

2. Blessings for Obedience

Prayer is not the only condition for receiving temporal blessings. *When we put God first in all things, He has promised to meet our material needs* (SCP 29, 83). This is what Jesus meant when He said, "But seek first His kingdom and His righteousness and all these things will be given to you as well" (Matthew 6:33).

When Jesus taught this principle, He was not referring to eternity but to the physical world in which these people lived. Paul affirmed this promise to the Corinthians when he was encouraging them to be generous in their giving. To reassure them, Paul followed his exhortation with this promise: "God is able to make all grace abound to you so that in all things at all times, *having all that you need*, you will abound in every good work" (2 Corinthians 9:8).

It is important to note that neither Jesus nor Paul was teaching "prosperity theology," the belief that God guarantees to multiply our material possessions if we are faithful givers. God has never promised that He will give us *more* than we need. However, He has promised to give us *what* we need.

3. Being Able to Be Generous

Probably no verse has been misinterpreted and misused more than Paul's statement: "You will be made rich in every way so that you can be generous on every occasion" (2 Corinthians 9:11*a*). If you want to accumulate material possessions, say some high-powered evangelists and so-called "prosperity theologians," then "sow your seed" and it will grow and multiply one hundredfold.

What did Paul mean? Some believe that he was not speaking of *material* possessions at all but rather of *spiritual* riches. But Paul seemingly had both in mind. If he were not speaking of material possessions, how could he say that these Corinthians would be able to "be generous on every occasion"? Furthermore, his agricultural analogy in verse 10 implies that Paul was talking about material blessings as a result of being generous with material gifts (2 Corinthians 9:10).

It seems, then, that Paul was teaching that if the Corinthians were generous, based upon their own resources, God would provide them with material blessings so they could continue to invest in the kingdom of God and see people come to Christ and grow in Christ. In this sense, they would be "enlarging the harvest of their righteousness." The focus here is not on what they would *receive* but on what they could *give* in order to do God's work in the world.

Paul may have also been speaking here of being rich in grace, meaning that because of God's gift of grace, they would be able to be "generous on every occasion" no matter what their economic situation. In this sense, they would be able to respond like the Macedonians, who actually gave out of poverty, which in God's sight was a "generous gift."

This interpretation is supported from Paul's earlier comment when he stated that "the *grace* that God had given the Macedonian churches" enabled them to give, and "out of the most severe trial, their overflowing joy and their extreme poverty welled up in *rich generosity*" (2 Corinthians 8:1-2). In other words, God's grace enabled these Christians to give even what they needed for themselves. Paul classified this as "rich generosity." This explanation, however, does not contradict the interpretation that Paul was also speaking of material blessings as well as of the gift of grace. In essence, Paul was teaching that *when Christians are generous, God has promised to enable them to continue to be generous* (SCP 84).

4. GENEROUS BLESSINGS

Paul shared another promise with the Corinthians: "Whoever sows sparingly, will also reap sparingly, and whoever sows generously will also reap generously" (2 Corinthians 9:6). This simply means that *Christians who are generous in their giving will receive generous blessings; conversely, Christians who are not generous in their giving will not receive generous blessings* (SCP 81).

Any farmer knows that if he sows seeds sparingly, he will reap a small harvest. Conversely, If he sows seeds generously, he will reap an abundant harvest. Paul used this agricultural experience to illustrate Christian giving. The analogy must be carefully interpreted and applied, however, since Paul was not referring to *quantity* but *quality*. When it comes to giving, God does not measure the seed by how much is actually sown. Rather, He measures how much is sown by what is *available* to sow. Paul was teaching what Christ taught when He referred to the widow in the temple, who actually gave more than those who gave much because she gave sacrificially rather than out of plenty.

Again, some have interpreted Paul's teaching on "sowing generously" and "reaping generously" to be a prosperity theology. As stated earlier, nowhere in Scripture are Christians taught to "give" so that they may "gain" earthly abundance. Rather, giving is to be motivated by an unselfish heart that is willing to share unconditionally with those in need, regardless of the monetary return. Furthermore, we must remember that God's generous blessings in response to generous giving include more than material possessions. It involves, for example, seeing others respond generously because we have been a model. There is always joy and satisfaction in knowing we have helped someone else draw closer to God and walk in His will more faithfully.

5. BEING HONORED

There is another earthly reward that should be given to Christians who are faithful in sharing their material possessions, especially when their stewardship involves unusual generosity. *They should be honored in special ways by others in the Body of Christ* (SCP 108).

We have seen this principle illustrated in the life of Barnabas. The apostles evidently changed his name to conform to his generous and unselfish spirit. There can be no greater honor. A name that means "Son of Encouragement" would be a constant reminder of the way Barnabas reflected the life of Jesus Christ.

Epaphroditus serves as another illustration. The Philippian believers sent this man to Rome to deliver a gift of money to Paul. When he arrived, he found that Paul needed encouragement and continual economic assistance. Rather than return to Philippi immediately, Epaphroditus decided to stay by his friend's side. He felt such a keen sense of responsibility to Paul that he nearly died in fulfilling that duty.

When Epaphroditus eventually returned to Philippi, probably carrying a letter to the church there, Paul made clear that this man should be given due recognition for his sacrificial service: "Welcome him back in the Lord with great joy, and *honor men like him*" (Philippians 2:29).

It appears that Epaphroditus was the primary elder/pastor in Philippi. If so, what Paul wrote to the Philippians has a direct application to spiritual leaders today. Many pastors devote most of their lives to helping others. Unfortunately, some neglect their own families to minister to the larger family of God. They often serve long hours. They are always on call. Their lives are not their own, with little privacy. They often work seven days a week, and in many instances, are not paid commensurate with their education, experience, and dedication as are many of their fellow Christians in the business world. And the majority of pastors I rub shoulders with do all this without complaining or feeling sorry for themselves. They have voluntarily chosen to be servants of Jesus Christ and others.

And yet these leaders are often the last to be shown special appreciation and honor. They are often taken for granted. Unfortunately, they are even misunderstood, misinterpreted, and criticized when they attempt to take some time off. And if they dare ask for a raise in salary, they are accused of being materialistic and self-serving. Sadly, Christians are too quick to point to those few spiritual leaders who have abused their sacred role and have taken advantage of others. Against the backdrop of a few unfaithful shepherds, they judge their own pastors.

There are exceptions, of course. Some churches practice this principle very well. And what a rewarding experience it is. All Christians need encouragement and honor for being faithful, especially when they share what they have in a sacrificial way. As believers, we should never withhold this earthly blessing from those who deserve it. God planned that it should happen. When it does not, we are simply being disobedient and withholding a blessing from others that God wants them to have.

6. CORPORATE BLESSINGS

As Christians who live in the Western world, we are so used to thinking in terms of individualism that we lose sight of the corporate nature of Christianity. Consequently, we tend to personalize all promises in the Bible and fail to realize that many promises are corporate in nature. This is true in the area of giving.

When Paul wrote to the Philippians, thanking them for their generous gifts, he said, "And my God will meet all your needs according to his glorious riches in Christ Jesus" (Philippians 4:19). He was confident that *not only would God meet the needs of the individual members of the church in Philippi but of the corporate body as well* (SCP 112). And in meeting their needs as a corporate body, He would also be meeting personal needs.

To be more specific, when a church is faithful in giving, God may choose to bless certain individuals in the church who, in turn, can help others in the church who are in need. In this sense, Paul's statement to the Corinthians applies to Christians within specific local churches as well as to churches helping other churches: "Our desire is not that others [other churches] might be relieved while you [as a church] are hard pressed, but that there might be equality" (2 Corinthians 8:13).

7. GLORIFYING GOD ETERNALLY

To this point, we have seen that it is not wrong for believers to be motivated to share their material possessions in hopes of receiving present blessings. However, we must realize that *the most important perspective in Scripture involves eternal blessings*. Our most significant rewards will not come in this life (Matthew 19:28-29; SCP 40).

Paul helps us understand more fully the concept of eternal rewards for faithful service. As Christians, we will "all appear before the judgment seat of Christ" (2 Corinthians 5:10; see also Romans 14:10 and Ephesians 6:8). When this happens, each Christian will "receive what is due him for the things done while in the body, whether good or bad" (2 Corinthians 5:10*b*).

The judgment seat of Christ will take place immediately following the coming of Christ for His church (1 Corinthians 4:5; 2 Timothy 4:8; Revelation 22:12; cf. Matthew 16:27; Luke 14:14). At that time the work of some Christians will be "burned up" because it is "wood, hay and straw" (1 Corinthians 3:12, 15). The work of other Christians will survive because they have built upon their foundation (namely, Jesus Christ) with "gold, silver and costly stones" (1 Corinthians 3:11, 14).

Though Paul was using figurative language, he was describing a real event. In other words, all true believers will inherit eternal life because of Christ's saving power (1 Corinthians 3:15). But some Christians will receive special rewards for being faithful, and other Christians will not receive any rewards because they have not been faithful.

How will we use these rewards? This question introduces us to another important biblical observation. According to the apostle John, all believers (probably symbolized by the twenty-four elders) will "lay their crowns before the throne and say: 'You are worthy, our Lord and God, to receive glory and honor and power, for you created all things, and by your will they were created and have their being'" (Revelation 4:10-11).

The total biblical perspective, then, is that our basic motivation as Christians in all that we do for Jesus Christ (including how we use our material possessions) should be to accumulate rewards and crowns, not to benefit ourselves. As we serve Jesus Christ throughout eternity, there will be no mixed motives—as we all have on earth because of our human condition—but our desire will only be to love and honor Jesus Christ for what He has done for us.

We must constantly remind ourselves of this higher and more noble eternal motive. Furthermore, we must be careful not to be enamored with a prosperity theology that contradicts this eternal perspective. God has not guaranteed that material blessings will come to us in this life if we are faithful givers. If that were true, the apostles would have sat on twelve thrones in Israel before they died. Furthermore, all the believers in Jerusalem would have received one hundred times what they had given up before they passed on to their eternal rewards.

But the facts are that those who became Christians in the early years of Christianity were eventually persecuted and driven out of Jerusalem. Some evidently lost what little they had left. And later, those who did have something left were wiped out by a severe famine. Tradition tells us that all but one of the apostles was martyred for the cause of Christ. Only John died a natural death—in exile—but certainly not a wealthy man.

These people *will* be rewarded. It will be a hundredfold for what they have given up for Christ's sake. We, too, will receive the same rewards in proportion to what we have given up for God's will and work. However, this promise in all of its fullness will be in God's eternal kingdom, when we inhabit the "new heaven" and the "new earth." And the primary purpose will be to serve Christ in special ways. It is not wrong to be motivated to be faithful stewards of our material possessions by this wonderful and marvelous eternal reality.

8. ETERNAL REWARDS FOR SACRIFICIAL GIVING

After Jesus observed the poor widow putting "two very small copper coins" into the temple treasury, He gathered His disciples around Him and used her gift as a visual illustration. "I tell you the truth," He said, "this poor widow has put more into the treasury than all the others. They all gave out of their wealth; but she, out of her poverty, put in everything—all she had to live on" (Mark 12:43-44).

With this observation, Jesus explained what He meant when He said that many who have given much, even as believers, "will be last" while "many who are last will be first" (Matthew 19:30). In God's scheme of things, "one hundredfold" in the eternal kingdom of God will be measured, not in terms of the *quantity* this widow gave but in terms of the *proportional* nature of the gift. She will receive much more from the Lord, according to His accounting system, than those who gave a lot and had a lot left over. As Alan Cole states, "It is well to remember that the Lord measures giving, not by what we give, but by what we keep for ourselves; and the widow kept nothing, but gave all."[1]

Jesus was teaching with this illustration that *God will reward Christians in His eternal kingdom on the basis of the degree of sacrifice involved in their giving* (SCP 33). This means that compared to many American Christians, there will be believers from other cultures of the world and from various moments in history (including New Testament Christians) who will be far more rewarded in God's kingdom. Put another way, many Christians in the kingdom of God, like the widow, have given out of their poverty. In some instances, they gave all "they had to live on."

Conversely, most of us Christians in America have given out of "plenty" rather than "poverty." This in no way means we have necessarily violated the will of God, especially if we give regularly and systematically. Rather, It simply means that there will be others inhabiting the kingdom who will be honored ahead of us. All of us will have eternal life, but some Christians will have far greater rewards and far greater prominence because of their sacrificial spirit. In certain situations, some of us will probably have had our rewards on earth (Matthew 6:2). Their rewards, however, will last throughout eternity.

NOTE

1. R. A. Cole, *The Gospel According to St. Mark: An Introduction and Commentary*, The Tyndale New Testament Commentaries, vol. 2 (Grand Rapids: Eerdmans, 1961), p. 196.

LET'S CHECK OURSELVES

On a scale of one to ten, circle the number that best represents how well you believe the people in your church or group practice the biblical principle found in each question.

1. Do the people in our church not only thank God for their material possessions but also ask Him to continue to meet their daily needs?

VERY LITTLE				SOMEWHAT				EXTENSIVELY	
1	2	3	4	5	6	7	8	9	10

2. Are the people in our church putting God first in all things and trusting Him to then meet their material needs?

VERY LITTLE				SOMEWHAT				EXTENSIVELY	
1	2	3	4	5	6	7	8	9	10

3. Are the believers in our church able to continue to give to God's work on a regular basis because they have already become faithful givers?

VERY LITTLE				SOMEWHAT				EXTENSIVELY	
1	2	3	4	5	6	7	8	9	10

4. Do Christians understand the fallacy of prosperity theology but, at the same time, understand the true nature of the blessings God wants to bestow on those who are faithful in their giving?

VERY LITTLE				SOMEWHAT				EXTENSIVELY	
1	2	3	4	5	6	7	8	9	10

5. Have we developed a sensitive way to honor people in our church who have made special sacrifices to help meet other people's economic needs?

VERY LITTLE				SOMEWHAT				EXTENSIVELY	
1	2	3	4	5	6	7	8	9	10

6. Do the people in our church understand that God desires to meet the needs of the whole church body, as well as individual needs within the body?

VERY LITTLE				SOMEWHAT				EXTENSIVELY	
1	2	3	4	5	6	7	8	9	10

7. Are the people in our church motivated to give in view of the fact that they will be able to glorify God throughout eternity because of their faithfulness on earth?

VERY LITTLE				SOMEWHAT				EXTENSIVELY	
1	2	3	4	5	6	7	8	9	10

8. Do the people in our church understand that eternal rewards will be based upon the degree to which they make special sacrifices in sharing their material possessions to further God's work?

VERY LITTLE				SOMEWHAT				EXTENSIVELY	
1	2	3	4	5	6	7	8	9	10

How to Use This Evaluation Exercise

1. Duplicate these eight questions on a separate sheet, and have each person in your group anonymously evaluate your church.
2. Tabulate the responses to find an average score. To do so, total the numbers circled in each question. Divide this total number by the number of people responding to that particular question. This will give you a "mean," or average, score.
3. Discover the greatest needs in your church by arranging the scores numerically from the highest to the lowest. Those scores that are lowest represent the areas that need immediate attention.
4. In discussing these scores and the principles involved, spend time first of all reviewing the areas of strength in your church. Spend time in prayer, thanking God for those strengths.
5. Finally, spend time discussing ways to practice the principles that are the most neglected in your church. The following questions will help:
   a. What are the areas of greatest need?
   b. What can we do that we are not doing to practice these biblical principles?
   c. What specific goals can we set up to practice these principles?
   d. What can we do *immediately*?

Personalize This Project

Follow the procedure described at the end of chapter 1.

9

Living in a Materialistic Culture

Few people question that we are living in a materialistic culture, particularly in the Western world. How can Christians live in this kind of society and yet not conform to its values? Following are both scriptural warnings against materialism and some positive biblical guidelines for rising above this kind of life-style.

1. Avoiding Materialistic Bondage

In His Sermon on the Mount, Jesus stated, "You cannot serve both God and money" (Matthew 6:24). This was the rich young ruler's tension point. Money had become his master. Jesus knew this to be true because He could penetrate the thoughts and intents of this man's heart. Unfortunately, he walked away sadly, not aware that he could master his money for the glory of God and experience great joy in doing so.

The rich young ruler represents those who do not respond to the gospel because of their materialistic bondage. But this poses a question. *Is it possible for a Christian to be in bondage as well? Unfortunately, the answer to this question is a decided "Yes!"* (SCP 28). Just as some Christians may be serving other carnal and sinful desires, as outlined by Paul in Galatians 5:19-20 (sexual immorality, impurity, jealousy), some are guilty of being in bondage to their material possessions.

If this is true in our lives, even to the slightest degree, we must not allow God's grace and patience to permit us to go on sinning. If we do, at some point in time, He will discipline us as a loving father. If we "are not disciplined, then" we "are illegitimate children and not true sons" (Hebrews 12:8).

How does God discipline His children when they serve their material possessions rather than Him? The most extreme form involves the way He dealt with Ananias and Sapphira. Fortunately, this is not God's normal form of discipline. But one aspect of God's discipline is certain. We will "reap what we sow" (Galatians 6:7). Though it may take years to harvest this painful crop, some materialistic parents experience it when their own children grow up and become even more materialistic than they are. What is worse, our children may become materialistic in the ultimate sense and, like the rich young ruler, reject Jesus Christ.

We must avoid materialistic bondage at all costs. To do so, we must present our bodies to Jesus Christ and renew our minds. We must, with an act of the will, put God first in all that we do. We must "seek first his kingdom and his righteousness" (Matthew 6:33).

2. GUARDING AGAINST DISHONEST LEADERS

Christianity and money are interrelated and inseparable entities. So *wherever Christianity is active, some will attempt to use the Christian message to benefit themselves* (SCP 43). This reality is verified again and again throughout the New Testament. As soon as the church of Jesus Christ was born, it was viewed as "big business" by men and women with selfish intentions. Simon the sorcerer even tried to "buy" the power of the Holy Spirit to enhance his own political and economic situation (Acts 8:19).

This kind of exploitation and abuse is one of the reasons Paul insisted that any person who was appointed as a spiritual leader in the church should not be "a lover of money" (1 Timothy 3:3) or an individual who was guilty of "pursuing dishonest gain" (1 Timothy 3:8; Titus 1:7). Peter affirmed the same concern when he exhorted the elders in various churches to "be shepherds of God's flock . . . *not greedy for money*, but eager to serve" (1 Peter 5:2).

Since we know there will be those who will seek positions in the Christian community with wrong motives, we must be careful, however, not to falsely judge and penalize honest Christian leaders. If we apply all the principles God has outlined for us in the area of using our material possessions, we will be able to face these problems and solve them. We will be discerning, and at the same time, be able to avoid either/or reactions. Most importantly, we must make sure that we ourselves are not guilty of utilizing Christianity in a self-serving way.

3. RESISTING TEMPTATIONS

The Bible does not teach that it is wrong in itself to have a large number of material possessions. However, *accumulating wealth brings with it specific temptations for both Christians and non-Christians* (SCP 60). When warning unconverted rich people against the power of money to keep them from responding to God's will, James concluded his thoughts by outlining three temptations that are applicable to Christians as well.

Christians can be tempted to accumulate more and more—to hoard wealth (James 5:3). They can also be tempted to be unfair, unethical, and dishonest. For instance, James refers to people who had "failed to pay the workmen" they hired to take care of their fields (James 5:4). The third temptation is to be self-indulgent. James accused certain rich people of having "lived on earth in luxury." They had "fattened themselves" for the "day of slaughter." They had prepared themselves for a tragic end. Unfortunately, Christians, too, can get caught in the self-indulgent trap.

As believers, we must be constantly on guard against all these temptations. This is particularly true in societies that provide people with economic opportunities—such as America. We can easily be tempted to love our money more than we love God. When we do, we have reversed God's plan. We are storing up treasures on earth rather than in heaven.

4. AVOIDING SELF-CENTERED BEHAVIOR

Shortly before he died, Paul wrote a letter to Timothy, exhorting him to warn Christians to avoid the increasing tendency to intensify love for self, money, and pleasure. "There will be terrible times in the last days," he wrote. "People will be lovers of themselves, lovers of money . . . lovers of pleasure rather than lovers of God—having a form of godliness but denying its power. Have nothing to do with them" (2 Timothy 3:1-2*a*, 4*b*-5).

As believers living in the twentieth century, we can quickly establish two facts. First, we are nearer to the second coming of Christ than ever before. If the time was near when Paul wrote his second letter to Timothy, how close is it nearly two thousand years later? Second, the world in general reflects the trends outlined by Paul. This is certainly true in American culture. Many people today are "lovers of themselves, lovers of money" and "lovers of pleasure rather than lovers of God" (2 Timothy 3:2, 4). Our society is manifesting these characteristics more every day.

There is only one solution to this problem. *As Christians, we must avoid the increasing tendency to intensify love for self, money, and pleasure* (SCP 119). We must be continually "transformed by the renewing" of our minds. It is only then that we will "be able to test and approve what God's will is—his good, pleasing and perfect will" (Romans 12:2). This is foundational to everything we do—including the way we view and use our material possessions.

5. GUARDING AGAINST SELF-DECEPTION AND RATIONALIZATION

The church in Laodicea is the last of the seven churches mentioned in Revelation. Though I do not hold dogmatically to the theory that the seven churches forecast the development of the church throughout history, I cannot deny that there appears to be a chronological unfolding of one basic truth: The imminence of Christ's return grows more prominent in the exhortations that are given from church to church (see Revelation 2:5, 16, 25; 3:3, 11, 20). Christ's final warning to the church in Laodicea seems to be related to the grand culmination of history upon His return: "Here I am! I stand at the door and knock" (Revelation 3:20*a*).

This church had a problem, and Jesus accused it: "You say, 'I am rich; I have acquired wealth and do not need a thing.' But you do not realize that you are wretched, pitiful, poor, blind and naked" (Revelation 3:17).

The state of this final church is one that reflects a materialistic mindset conformed to the world's system. Jesus Christ made clear that it is possible to be lulled into complacency and a carnal state by cultural affluence. *Christians must be on guard against this kind of self-deception and rationalization* (SCP 126).

Unfortunately, this kind of behavior has already permeated American society. Never have we had more materially but never have we as Christians given so little to the Lord's work. We are told that the average Christian gives only 2 percent of his earnings to the Lord. Something is desperately wrong. We are violating the Word of God. We are not giving from our "firstfruits" systematically, regularly, and proportionately. If Jews under the Old Testament law gave an average of 23 percent of their annual income to do the work of God, how much should the average American Christian be giving to be a proportionate giver?

Like the Laodicean Christians, we need three things: "gold refined in the fire"; "white clothes to wear"; and "salve to put on" our eyes (Revelation 3:18). Gold symbolizes faith (1 Peter 1:7). White garments symbolize true righteousness and holiness (Revelation 19:8). Salve for our eyes illustrates a restored vision—to be able to see clearly how materialistic we have become. The good news is that Jesus is saying there is hope for churches that have become Laodicean in nature. We can be restored and renewed.

6. Using Our Excess Creatively

How can we avoid getting trapped in materialism? Jesus has given us some specific and positive guidelines: "Do not store up for yourselves treasures on earth, but store up for yourselves treasures in heaven" (Matthew 6:19).

On one occasion, Jesus told the story of a wealthy farmer whose land was very productive, so much so that he decided to tear down his granaries and build larger ones. He was satisfied with his material accumulations and concluded that he had enough resources to retire. Unfortunately, he did not realize that he was suddenly going to die. He had made preparation for this life but not for eternity. Jesus then made an application that is directly related to His teaching in the Sermon on the Mount: "This is how it will be with anyone who stores up things for himself but is not rich toward God" (Luke 12:21).

Jesus clearly taught that *whatever excess material possessions God enables Christians to accumulate should be used in creative ways to further the kingdom of God* (SCP 26). This is an important way to avoid getting trapped in materialism.

This does not mean it is wrong to institute a plan to care for ourselves and our families in the future. Many teachings in the book of Proverbs affirm that we are to be responsible Christians (see Proverbs 6:6-8; 10:5; 13:22*a*; 21:5; 24:27; 27:23; 28:19). What, then, was Jesus teaching when He told us not to store up "treasures on earth" but rather to store up "treasures in heaven"? He was dealing with our priorities. All that we do should be focused on eternal values. Those of us who have much should give much—as Paul says—in proportion to what we have. In this way, we will be using our excess to accomplish God's will in the world.

This leads to some pertinent and pointed questions. What is excessive in terms of the kinds of houses we live in, the kinds of cars we drive, or the clothes we wear? What is ample in terms of planning for future needs, including retirement? How much insurance should we have? How much should we plan to leave for our children or even for our grandchildren?

In some cultures, these questions are answered automatically. People live and die with just enough to meet their needs. However, in affluent areas of the world, sincere Christians face these questions everyday.

There are no pat answers. These questions must be addressed at a personal level by every Christian or Christian couple. The principles outlined in this study will enable Christians in all cultural situations to answer these questions satisfactorily, assuming that we take them seriously and providing we are honest with God and ourselves.

7. Resting in God's Faithfulness

Another positive guideline for avoiding a materialistic mind-set is to entrust our present and future needs to God. Jesus taught, "Do not worry about tomorrow, for tomorrow will worry about itself" (Matthew 6:34*a*).

Jesus did not intend for His followers to be unconcerned about their material needs. In fact, the very moment He was teaching these people not to "worry about tomorrow," His earthly father was probably hard at work in his carpenter shop earning a living to support the rest of the family. And as we have already observed, several of Jesus' parables emphasized diligent planning, hard work, and responsibility as citizens.

Jesus was dealing with our human tendency to devote all our energies to worrying about our earthly existence: what we "will eat or drink," or what we "will wear" (Matthew 6:25). He encouraged His listeners to "look at the birds of the air" and to look at "the lilies of the field" (Matthew 6:26, 28). If our Father in heaven takes care of the birds and the flowers, will He not take care of His own children? After all, Jesus said, "the pagans run after all these things, and your heavenly Father knows that you need them" (Matthew 6:32).

Jesus was teaching us that *it is not the Father's will for Christians to be absorbed with worry about the future and how their material needs will be met* (SCP 30). This principle, of course, does not conflict with Paul's exhortation to be a responsible Christian and to work for a living (2 Thessalonians 3:6-10). However, if we are continually anxious, we have probably not arrived at that important balance between trusting God to meet our needs and, at the same time, doing our part to be responsible Christians in the world.

8. Refocusing Our Values

Unfortunately, when all is well, we tend to drift away from God's perspective on material possessions. When we do, *God sometimes allows difficulties and discomforts to come into our lives to assist us in reestablishing our priorities on eternal values* (SCP 42, 120).

This is illustrated in the church in Jerusalem. They had a limited theological perspective that caused them to be satisfied with their present environment. Consequently, God allowed persecution to force the Christians out of Jerusalem so that they would take the Lord's commission seriously to "make disciples of all nations" (Matthew 28:19).

Years later, the apostle Peter wrote to the suffering church that was "scattered throughout Pontus, Galatia, Cappadocia, Asia and Bithynia" (1 Peter 1:1). He encouraged them to rejoice, even though they were suffering "grief and all kinds of trials. These have come," Peter explained, "so that your faith—of greater worth than gold which perishes even though refined by fire—may be proved genuine and may result in praise, glory and honor when Jesus Christ is revealed" (1 Peter 1:6-7).

We must not misunderstand this principle. God does not purposely set out to hurt His children. Neither is He responsible for sinful actions, such as the behavior of men like the Emperor Nero who was probably responsible for Paul's death and, perhaps, Peter's as well. No one can blame God for this evil man's actions. He operated with his own volition. But the fact remains that God is sovereign and He can even use evil to achieve good things (Genesis 50:20).

Will God allow persecution to come to America to cause Christians to refocus their values? If He does, it will not be out of harmony with what we see in the lives of Christians throughout the history of the church. In the meantime, we have a choice. We do not have to conform to the values of this world. We can internalize and practice the principles of the Word of God, no matter what happens in our society.

9. LEARNING TO BE CONTENT

The apostle Paul gives another positive principle for avoiding the materialistic trap. He demonstrated it with his own life when he was in a Roman prison: "I know what it is to be in need, and I know what it is to have plenty. *I have learned the secret of being content* in any and every situation, whether well fed or hungry, whether living in plenty or in want" (Philippians 4:12).

Paul had an unusual capacity to adapt to various situations and circumstances and still reflect contentment (2 Corinthians 11:23–12:10). The "situations" that he wrote about in his letter included his material needs—being "well fed or hungry," and "living in plenty or in want."

Paul's point is that *we should learn to be content in the difficult times as well as in the prosperous times* (SCP 110). It is true that God has promised to meet our needs. However, this does not mean that we will always have everything we need to make life comfortable. It is one thing to be happy and content when we have food on our table, clothes on our back, shelter over our heads, and some money in the bank. But what if all these things were missing? How content would we be? How would we adapt? In the midst of these kinds of pressures, we must also remember that God may be allowing these difficulties to refocus our values.

10. SEEKING TO BE GODLY

Paul hit the problem of materialism head on when he wrote to Timothy: "the love of money is the root of all kinds of evil. Some people, eager for money, have wandered from the faith and pierced themselves with many griefs" (1 Timothy 6:10). When Christians set their goals to become rich rather than to become godly (1 Timothy 6:6), they are headed for serious trouble. Unfortunately, they will not find contentment. And if their focus is wealth, they will not be able to resist the temptations that invariably come their way. They will eventually find themselves in "a trap." They will be controlled by many "foolish and harmful desires that plunge men into ruin and destruction" (1 Timothy 6:9). It is in this context that Paul wrote about the love of money being "the root of all kinds of evil."

All Christians should set as their foremost goal to be godly and contented people—to "seek first his kingdom and his righteousness" (Matthew 6:33*a*; SCP 117). If they do, everything else will come into focus. As Jesus said, "all these things will be given to you as well" (Matthew 6:33*b*). If God brings wealth and prosperity, we will be able to handle the temptations that come with these blessings—if we use what God gives us not only to meet our own basic needs but to also use our excess in creative ways to invest in God's eternal kingdom. That is why Paul also told Timothy to "command" the rich "to do good, to be rich in good deeds, and to be generous and willing to share" (1 Timothy 6:18).

LET'S CHECK OURSELVES

On a scale of one to ten, circle the number that best represents how well you believe the people in your church or group practice the biblical principle found in each question.

1. Are the people in our church in bondage to their material possessions?

VERY LITTLE				SOMEWHAT				EXTENSIVELY	
1	2	3	4	5	6	7	8	9	10

2. Are there people in our local church or community who are using the message of Christianity primarily to benefit themselves?

VERY LITTLE				SOMEWHAT				EXTENSIVELY	
1	2	3	4	5	6	7	8	9	10

3. Do the Christians in our church understand the subtle temptations that accompany the accumulation of material possessions?

VERY LITTLE				SOMEWHAT				EXTENSIVELY	
1	2	3	4	5	6	7	8	9	10

4. Do the Christians in our church realize that they can be easily influenced away from the will of God by the materialistic and hedonistic philosophies prominent in our culture today?

VERY LITTLE				SOMEWHAT				EXTENSIVELY	
1	2	3	4	5	6	7	8	9	10

5. Are the people in our church self-deceived by the materialistic philosophy that permeates our culture, causing them to rationalize away their selfishness and lack of generosity?

VERY LITTLE				SOMEWHAT				EXTENSIVELY	
1	2	3	4	5	6	7	8	9	10

6. Do the people in our church use their excess material possessions in creative ways to carry out God's work in the world?

VERY LITTLE				SOMEWHAT				EXTENSIVELY	
1	2	3	4	5	6	7	8	9	10

7. Are the people in our church anxious and worried about their material needs?

VERY LITTLE				SOMEWHAT				EXTENSIVELY	
1	2	3	4	5	6	7	8	9	10

8. To what extent has God allowed difficulties to come into the lives of the people in our church to help refocus priorities on eternal values?

VERY LITTLE				SOMEWHAT				EXTENSIVELY	
1	2	3	4	5	6	7	8	9	10

9. Are the believers in our church demonstrating contentment when they face difficult financial times?

VERY LITTLE				SOMEWHAT				EXTENSIVELY	
1	2	3	4	5	6	7	8	9	10

10. Are the people in our church seeking to be godly rather than to accumulate wealth?

VERY LITTLE				SOMEWHAT				EXTENSIVELY	
1	2	3	4	5	6	7	8	9	10

HOW TO USE THIS EVALUATION EXERCISE

1. Duplicate these ten questions on a separate sheet, and have each person in your group anonymously evaluate your church.
2. Tabulate the responses to find an average score. To do so, total the numbers circled in each question. Divide this total number by the number of people responding to that particular question. This will give you a "mean," or average, score.
3. Discover the greatest needs in your church by arranging the scores numerically from the highest to the lowest. Those scores that are lowest represent the areas that need immediate attention.
4. In discussing these scores and the principles involved, spend time first of all reviewing the areas of strength in your church. Spend time in prayer, thanking God for those strengths.
5. Finally, spend time discussing ways to practice the principles that are the most neglected in your church. The following questions will help:
    a. What are the areas of greatest need?
    b. What can we do that we are not doing to practice these biblical principles?
    c. What specific goals can we set up to practice these principles?
    d. What can we do *immediately*?

PERSONALIZE THIS PROJECT

Follow the procedure described at the end of chapter 1.

10

Supporting Spiritual Leaders

In chapter 5, we noted that a predominant theme in Scripture is that Christians should share their material possessions to meet human needs. We are to care for needy parents, help the poor, and share with people in crisis. As a church, we are responsible to make sure this happens in a fair, equitable, and organized fashion.

In this chapter, we will see that the Word of God becomes even more specific. We are to make sure that those who devote great segments of their time to the ministry are cared for financially, "especially those whose work is preaching and teaching" (1 Timothy 5:17). The Holy Spirit has given definite guidelines, both for "those who give" and for "those who receive." The first eight principles in this chapter deal with those who give; the remaining five concern those who receive.

1. JESUS' FOUNDATIONAL TEACHINGS ON GIVING

Jesus Christ taught that if people want to be honored and rewarded by God, they should honor and reward those who devote their time and effort to Christian ministry. This is what He meant when He said, "if anyone gives even a cup of cold water to one of these *little ones* because he is my disciple, I tell you the truth, he will certainly not lose his reward" (Matthew 10:42).

The context for this statement involves a charge that Jesus gave to the twelve disciples when He sent them out to teach, to confront demonic activity, and to heal physical illnesses (Matthew 10:1). They were "not to take along any gold or silver or copper." They were to take "no bag for the journey, or extra tunic, or sandals or a staff." These men were to be supported by those to whom they ministered. Jesus then made this point clear: "The worker is worth his keep" (Matthew 10:9-10). If people ministered to the apostles in a physical and material way—even if it involved only "a cup of cold water"—they would be rewarded by God Himself.

When the apostles embarked on this missionary journey, they did not wear colorful robes like the religious leaders in Israel. Neither did they arrive in various cities and towns with pomp and circumstance. They had no money in their pockets and did not even carry a suitcase with extra clothes. From the world's point of view, they were poor and unworthy. Thus, Jesus identified them as "little ones."

When Jesus referred to rewards for caring for His disciples, He was establishing an important principle: *God honors Christians in a special way when they meet the material needs of those who truly serve God* (SCP 31). Christians who care for their spiritual leaders' physical needs will not only encourage these people, they will also be blessed themselves—even if they can give only a little help from meager resources.

2. Paul's Foundational Teachings on Giving

On their first missionary journey, Paul and Barnabas "appointed elders" in several of the churches they founded (Acts 14:23). It may have been upon his return that Paul wrote his letter to the Galatians.[1] As he concluded this epistle, he gave this exhortation: "Anyone who receives instruction in the Word must share all good things with his instructor" (Galatians 6:6).

These new believers in the Galatian region needed to understand their financial responsibilities to those who ministered to them spiritually. These leaders were devoting great segments of their time to the ministry and needed material support so that they could care for their personal and family needs.

But Paul may have penned these words for another pragmatic reason. He referred to the *accountability* that goes with responsibility when he wrote to Timothy: "Do your best to present yourself to God as *one approved*, a workman who does not need to be ashamed and who *correctly handles* the word of truth" (2 Timothy 2:15). To teach the Word of God effectively takes a great deal of time and effort, especially if it is done in a manner that is well-pleasing to God. So, when Paul wrote "The worker deserves his wages" (1 Timothy 5:18; Luke 10:7), he was simply repeating the words of Jesus. If elders work long hours preparing to teach and then teaching, they need financial assistance. This is every local church's responsibility before God (see SCP 61).

3. Giving "Double Honor"

When Paul later wrote to Timothy, he expanded on what he had said to the Galatian Christians. He emphasized that pastors and teachers who are hardworking, efficient, and productive in the ministry should also be rewarded accordingly: "The elders who direct the affairs of the church well are worthy of double honor, especially those whose work is preaching and teaching" (1 Timothy 5:17).

The Greek word *time* (translated "honor" in this verse) refers to remuneration or honoraria. The word for "double" connotes generous, or ample, financial support.[2] In other words, the amount of support should be contingent on how well spiritual leaders carry out their duties (see SCP 116). Once again, Paul was concerned for those who devote a great deal of time to "preaching and teaching" the Word of God, which correlates with the directive he gave to the Galatians.

This principle indicates that God has not eliminated from human nature the need for earthly recognition. One of the most motivating rewards, even for Christian workers, is financial remuneration that reflects appreciation for a job well done. In this sense, the Scriptures promote "merit pay." Paul established the principle with the analogy, "the hardworking farmer should be the first to receive a share of the crops" (2 Timothy 2:6).

4. CREATING JOY AND HAPPINESS THROUGH GIVING

"I thank my God every time I remember you. In all my prayers for all of you, I always pray with joy because of your partnership in the gospel from the first day until now" (Philippians 1:3-5). Paul wrote this from a Roman prison. Anyone in the ministry whose physical needs are faithfully being met by fellow Christians can identify with Paul's experience when he wrote this letter. He joyfully thanked God every time he remembered the Philippians because they had been his partners in the gospel from the first day people came to Christ in Philippi. Here the term "partners" refers primarily to fellowship with Paul through financial support.

Lydia was Paul's first convert. When she became a Christian, she immediately insisted that he and his fellow missionaries (Silas, Timothy, and Luke) stay in her home, using it as a base for their ministry in Philippi (Acts 16:15). In fact, her home probably became the first permanent meeting place for the church.

What can we learn from this biblical example? The principle is clear: *Believers who faithfully support God's servants in material ways create unusual joy and happiness in the hearts of those who receive their gifts* (SCP 106). All Christians should plan their giving with this truth in mind. Not only do we cause God's heart to rejoice, but we do the same for those we support. This is why Paul closed his letter to the Philippians by saying, "I rejoice greatly in the Lord that at last you have renewed your concern for me" (Philippians 4:10*a*).

5. Enriching Your Pastor's Prayer Life Through Giving

Another closely related principle comes from this same passage in Paul's letter to the Philippians. *Christians who faithfully support God's servants in material ways also enrich those people's prayer lives. Prayer becomes a joyful and exciting experience*: "I always pray with joy" (Philippians 1:3-4; SCP 107). This is how the Philippians' gifts affected Paul's prayer life. It will do the same for your pastor.

Only those who receive financial support from those they minister to can identify with this reality. I am well aware of how faithful givers have brought joy to my own prayer life over the years. This is true, not only when my own personal and family needs are met but when gifts are given to carry on the many aspects of ministry.

On occasion Christian business people have invited me to lunch to inform me that God had just blessed them in a financial way, generating rather large sums of money. They wanted to invest a portion of it in the ministry and asked me where it could best be used. Most of these experiences happened at a time of unique need for expanding the ministry. What joy I experienced at those times, and later, when I lifted my heart to God with a prayer of thanksgiving for these dedicated Christian men and women.

6. Forming a Financial Policy on Giving

Some Christians have used the "preaching tour" of the apostles (see the first principle in this chapter) as a model for sending out missionaries and Christian workers today. This is unfortunate since these isolated instances were never intended to give us specific methodology for supporting Christian workers.

As far as we know, Christ sent these groups out without provisions for their material needs on only one occasion. Further, these were not "extended tours." They soon returned to report on what had happened and once again operated under more normal economic conditions.

This observation does not invalidate "the principle of faith" when it comes to trusting God to meet our material needs. However, we must apply the principle of faith in the context of other principles in the Bible that relate to meeting material needs. Otherwise, Christian workers who need support can presume upon God and others. Conversely, those who should support Christian leaders can neglect their God-given responsibilities. Both mistakes can lead to incredible hurt, anxiety, insecurity, misunderstanding, and disillusionment.

What God is teaching us, then, is that *economic policies for meeting the physical needs of Christian leaders who devote their full time to ministry must be built upon the totality of God's Word* (SCP 39). The guidelines in this chapter can help in the development of such economic policies.

7. BEING ON GUARD AGAINST FALSE TEACHERS

Satan is a master at twisting truth. Soon after Paul had instructed Christians to take good care of their spiritual leaders economically, he and others had to warn against false teachers who would take advantage of people. Peter spoke pointedly to this issue when he wrote, "In their greed these [false] teachers will exploit you with stories they have made up" (2 Peter 2:3*a*). Jude added, "These men are blemishes at your love feasts, eating with you without the slightest qualm—shepherds who feed only themselves" (Jude 12*a*).

Note that the greed or covetousness referred to in these New Testament passages includes more than a lust for money. It also includes power and pleasure—especially sexual gratification. These three selfish and insidious motives (money, power, and sex), which are so prevalent today, revealed themselves from the very early years of the church. Furthermore, these false motives are based on dishonesty, which combine to form a subtle means to exploit Christians with fabricated stories (see SCP 122).

In today's society, Christians should be on guard against the same tactics. I have read enough "fund raising" appeals while being privy to the actual facts to know that some of these letters have been written by "experts." They contain stories designed to move people emotionally—stories that are exaggerated. Though some of these reports contain "half truths," they are fabricated nevertheless.

Does this mean that it is wrong to tell stories to motivate people to give and share their material possessions? Not at all. We need to know what the needs are, and there is no better way to communicate a need than to share a real-life event. However, the story must be true in all respects.

Is it inappropriate to send out fund-raising letters? Again, the answer is no. Unfortunately, however, "experts in the field" have discovered that people often do not respond to the simple facts. Sadly, many people have to be exposed to a crisis or something very dramatic before they will respond financially. Thus, the experts have learned how to get people to "open their pocketbooks." If there is no real crisis, part of the strategy is to create one. Or they will fabricate a breathtaking story, emphasizing particularly the dramatic aspects of conversion to Christ. At this point, some play the "numbers game"—publicizing how many decisions were made for Christ—when the statistics represent superficial and meaningless responses to the gospel.

A Christian today should never respond to fund-raising letters or any form of appeal without knowing a great deal about the circumstances. This includes having a good awareness of the reputation of those who are involved. If Christians violate these cautions, they will respond to needs that do not exist and give money to organizations that are not accountable for the way they spend the money.

It is also unfortunate that Christians who respond to these appeals are often neglecting their responsibility to support their own spiritual leaders who are truly in need and who will not resort to these kinds of tactics. This is perhaps the greater tragedy, discouraging to Christian leaders who are attempting to abide by the principles of Scripture.

8. EVALUATING A LEADER'S BELIEFS ABOUT JESUS CHRIST

Christians should never support religious teachers and leaders who claim to be Christians but who deny the deity of Jesus Christ. This is what the apostle John meant when he wrote: "If anyone comes to you and does not bring this teaching [that Jesus Christ has come in the flesh], do not take him into your house or welcome him. Anyone who welcomes him shares in his wicked work" (2 John 10-11).

John was not addressing the issue of private hospitality per se. Rather, he had in mind participants in a *house church.* In other words, Christians are not to officially welcome this kind of person to address the church body. To do so would be to expose believers to what John earlier identified as a "deceiver" and an "antichrist" (2 John 7).

Does this mean that Christians should never invite a representative from a religious group inside their homes who does not believe that Jesus Christ is God? Not at all. What John was teaching is that we should not open our home (and particularly our church) to show hospitality to false teachers. Providing material support is different from simply inviting a person into your home to discuss the Scriptures. The first involves encouraging this person to promote false doctrine, which John warns against. The second involves attempting to win this person to Jesus Christ, which the whole of Scripture supports.

Applied more specifically to the twentieth-century world, this principle means that *Christians should not be in association and fellowship with Christian leaders who do not teach the truth regarding Jesus Christ* (SCP 124). For example, Christians should not associate with a church where the leaders do not teach the deity of Christ. And by all means, they certainly should not give their money to support a church or organization that claims to be Christian but whose leaders and teachers deny that Jesus Christ is God.

This, of course, provides another guideline for our giving. To be worthy of financial support, people and organizations must be above reproach in the kind of life-style they promote *and* they must be correct in what they believe and teach.

9. LOOKING TO CHRISTIANS FOR FINANCIAL SUPPORT

Christian leaders should look to fellow Christians for financial support and not to the unbelievers they are attempting to reach with the gospel (SCP 63). The apostle Paul stands out as a clear model when it comes to fleshing out this principle. Reflecting on his ministry in Thessalonica, he wrote, "Surely you remember, brothers, our toil and hardship; we worked night and day in order not to be a burden to anyone while we preached the gospel of God to you" (1 Thessalonians 2:9).

In some instances, Paul applied this principle in his ministry to new Christians as well. Though the Thessalonians quickly joined the other Macedonian churches in becoming some of his most ardent financial supporters, Paul was cautious in receiving money from these new believers until they were sufficiently taught the true meaning of the gospel and also understood his own heart motives (1 Thessalonians 2:9-10).

This principle has at least three points of application for Christian leaders today. First, people who desire to have a vocational Christian ministry should look to believers for financial support. Second, Christians who seek support for their ministry should look first and foremost to Christians they have ministered to spiritually. They should at least establish their reputation in some substantial way so that they are indeed workers who "deserve their wages" (1 Timothy 5:18). And third, those who are spiritual leaders in local churches should make sure they teach Christians their God-given responsibility—as Paul did.

10. GIVING UP FINANCIAL RIGHTS

Even though God has commanded that spiritual leaders be cared for financially by those they minister to, there are times when it is the part of wisdom for spiritual leaders to give up that right (SCP 67). Paul modeled this principle for us: "In the same way, the Lord has commanded that those who preach the gospel should receive their living from the gospel. *But I have not used any of those rights*" (1 Corinthians 9:14-15a).

When Paul applied this principle, he was not suggesting that other spiritual leaders were out of the will of God if they did not give up this right. However, no action on the part of a Christian leader demonstrates more dramatically purity of motive and concern for God's reputation than giving up money that belongs to them by divine decree. May God give us more spiritual leaders who are willing to avoid actions that might become a stumbling block to both unbelievers and immature Christians.

11. Feeling Free to Ask for Money

Paul illustrated that *Christian leaders should not hesitate to ask for help when there is a need, either for others or for themselves* (SCP 101). When he wrote to his good friend, Philemon, he made his request clear:

> I do wish, brother, that I may have some benefit from you in the Lord; refresh my heart in Christ. Confident of your obedience, I write to you, knowing that you will do even more than I ask. And one thing more: Prepare a guest room for me, for I hope to be restored to you in answer to your prayers. (Philemon 20-22)

In some respects Paul was out of character when he asked Philemon for personal help. On the other hand, he illustrates that Christians have a right to make their needs known. Though he was certainly cautious and sensitive, he was also direct.

This personal request correlates with the principle we have just noted and that Paul practiced consistently. He looked to those he had ministered to in a special way for his financial support. This factor is dominant in his letter to Philemon and explains why Paul took this freedom.

12. Storing Up Treasures for Others

When Paul wrote and thanked the Philippians for their gifts of money, he explained: "Not that I am looking for a gift, but I am looking for what may be *credited to your account*" (Philippians 4:17). According to R. P. Martin, Paul used an analogy here to communicate how he felt about the gifts the Philippians had sent him. He referred to a "fruitful investment" that "gained interest." These terms were used by people involved in lending institutions in Paul's day.

> What the Philippians gave as their gift was like an investment which would pay rich dividends in the service of the kingdom, as accumulating interest (*karpos*) stands to the credit (*logos*) of the depositor. At the last day, such generous and unstinted service which expressed itself in practical monetary support would not go unrecognized or unrewarded.[3]

Christians who support spiritual leaders in the ministry are accumulating special rewards in heaven based on the fruit that results. But the specific lesson we learn from Paul is that those who are supported by others should serve the Lord with this in mind. *Part of our motivation should be to accumulate eternal rewards for those who support us financially* (SCP 111). Paul appears more excited about what was being credited to the Philippians' account in heaven than he was about the gifts he had received to meet his own personal needs (Philippians 4:17).

13. Guarding Against Selfishness

Tucked away in a little letter we call 3 John is a powerful principle: *Those who receive their financial support from the church they serve must be on guard against selfishness that causes them to refuse to share financial help with other Christian leaders outside their church who are in need* (SCP 125).

In this third letter, the apostle commended Gaius for practicing hospitality toward true Christian workers. Furthermore, John publicly exposed another church leader named Diotrephes who violated this principle. This man actually refused to welcome the apostle John, and even excommunicated Christians from the church who attempted to practice the principle of hospitality (3 John 9-10). Diotrephes's motives and actions were based on unadulterated selfishness. Thus, John wrote, he "loves to be first" (3 John 9*a*).

Unfortunately, there are Diotrepheses in some churches today—pastors and other Christian leaders who become self-oriented and refuse to support other leaders and organizations simply because they want more for themselves. True, there must be balance here. For example, it is not right for a church to increase its missionary budget while neglecting to care for the financial needs of those who are ministering to them. But, when pastors develop a self-oriented approach to church finances and stand in the way of helping others, they are contradicting the very heart of the Christian message. It is an ultimate form of hypocrisy. May God give us more spiritual leaders like Gaius and fewer like Diotrephes.

Notes

1. Well-known scholars disagree as to *when* Galatians was written and to *whom*. J. B. Lightfoot, *St. Paul's Epistle to the Galatians*, 10th ed. (London: Macmillan and Co., 1890), pp. 18-35, believes the letter was written after Paul's second missionary journey through northern Galatia. On the other hand, Sir William Ramsay, *An Historical Commentary on St. Paul's Epistle to the Galatians* (New York: G. P. Putnam's Sons, 1900), pp. ii, 478, has contended that "the churches of Galatia" were those of Antioch, Pisidia, Iconium, Derbe, and Lystra, churches Paul established on his first missionary journey through southern Galatia. Merrill C. Tenney, *New Testament Survey* (Grand Rapids: Eerdmans, 1953), pp. 266-67, correctly states that "the importance of the difference of interpretation is that the southern Galatian theory allows for an earlier dating of Galatians and for a better explanation of its historical setting."

2. Donald Guthrie, *The Pastoral Epistles: An Introduction and Commentary*, The Tyndale New Testament Commentaries, vol. 14 (Grand Rapids: Eerdmans, 1957), p. 105.

3. Ralph P. Martin, *The Epistle of Paul to the Philippians: An Introduction and Commentary*, The Tyndale New Testament Commentaries, vol. 11, p. 181.

Let's Check Ourselves

On a scale of one to ten, circle the number that best represents how well you believe the people in your church or group practice the biblical principle found in each question.

1. Do the people in our church understand that God will honor them in a special way when they meet the material needs of their spiritual leaders?

VERY LITTLE   SOMEWHAT   EXTENSIVELY

1   2   3   4   5   6   7   8   9   10

2. Do the people in our church consider it a priority in their giving to financially support their pastors who faithfully teach them the Word of God?

VERY LITTLE   SOMEWHAT   EXTENSIVELY

1   2   3   4   5   6   7   8   9   10

3. Does our church reward our spiritual leaders financially for their hard work, especially in teaching the Word of God?

VERY LITTLE   SOMEWHAT   EXTENSIVELY

1   2   3   4   5   6   7   8   9   10

4. Do the people in our church realize how much joy and happiness they create in their spiritual leaders' hearts when they are faithful in their giving?

VERY LITTLE   SOMEWHAT   EXTENSIVELY

1   2   3   4   5   6   7   8   9   10

5. Do the people in our church realize the extent to which they enrich their spiritual leaders' prayer lives when they are faithful in their giving?

VERY LITTLE   SOMEWHAT   EXTENSIVELY

1   2   3   4   5   6   7   8   9   10

6. Have we developed our pastoral and missionary support policy on a biblical theology of giving that grows out of the totality of Scripture?

VERY LITTLE   SOMEWHAT   EXTENSIVELY

1   2   3   4   5   6   7   8   9   10

7. Are the Christians in our church aware of the questionable fund-raising schemes that are used in today's Christian world?

VERY LITTLE   SOMEWHAT   EXTENSIVELY

1   2   3   4   5   6   7   8   9   10

8. Have Christians in our church learned to discern when so-called spiritual leaders appear to be Bible-believing yet do not believe that Jesus Christ is truly God?

VERY LITTLE				SOMEWHAT				EXTENSIVELY	
1	2	3	4	5	6	7	8	9	10

9. Does our church encourage members who are interested in missionary work to develop ministry and serving relationships with Christians before they seek financial support?

VERY LITTLE				SOMEWHAT				EXTENSIVELY	
1	2	3	4	5	6	7	8	9	10

10. Are the spiritual leaders in our church committed to avoiding any activity that could be interpreted by unbelievers or immature Christians as taking unfair advantage of people financially?

VERY LITTLE				SOMEWHAT				EXTENSIVELY	
1	2	3	4	5	6	7	8	9	10

11. Do the people, and especially the leaders, in our church make it easy for our staff people to communicate their special economic needs through proper channels?

VERY LITTLE				SOMEWHAT				EXTENSIVELY	
1	2	3	4	5	6	7	8	9	10

12. Do the Christian leaders in our church realize they are storing up treasures in heaven not only for themselves because of faithful service but also for those who support them financially?

VERY LITTLE				SOMEWHAT				EXTENSIVELY	
1	2	3	4	5	6	7	8	9	10

13. Are our spiritual leaders teaching and leading us to use some of our church income to help other Christian leaders and ministries?

VERY LITTLE				SOMEWHAT				EXTENSIVELY	
1	2	3	4	5	6	7	8	9	10

How to Use This Evaluation Exercise

1. Duplicate these thirteen questions on a separate sheet, and have each person in your group anonymously evaluate your church.

2. Tabulate the responses to find an average score. To do so, total the numbers circled in each question. Divide this total number by the number of people responding to that particular question. This will give you a "mean," or average, score.

3. Discover the greatest needs in your church by arranging the scores numerically from the highest to the lowest. Those scores that are lowest represent the areas that need immediate attention.

4. In discussing these scores and the principles involved, spend time first of all reviewing the areas of strength in your church. Spend time in prayer, thanking God for those strengths.

5. Finally, spend time discussing ways to practice the principles that are the most neglected in your church. The following questions will help:
   a. What are the areas of greatest need?
   b. What can we do that we are not doing to practice these biblical principles?
   c. What specific goals can we set up to practice these principles?
   d. What can we do *immediately*?

Personalize This Project

Follow the procedure described at the end of chapter 1.

11

God's Specific Plan for Giving

God outlines for Christians of all time a definite plan for giving. Though the New Testament approach is based on broad *divine principles* (rather than on a *detailed pattern* as it was for Israel), it is nevertheless specific and comprehensive. Because it is based on principles, God's New Testament plan crosses all cultural and economic boundaries. It worked in Jerusalem, Antioch, Thessalonica, and Corinth, whether the church was composed primarily of Jewish believers or Gentile Christians, or a roughly equal mix. It worked wherever the church existed, throughout the Roman world. Therefore, it will work in an affluent society in the Western world or in a deprived community in a Third World country. It is supracultural and relevant any place in the world and at any moment in history.

1. "EACH ACCORDING TO HIS ABILITY"

New Testament writers have made clear that God's plan is for all Christians to be involved in sharing their material possessions to carry on God's work in the world. This principle was first modeled in Jerusalem. The same dynamic can be seen in the church at Antioch when a severe famine left the Christians in Judea in serious need. The Christians in this Gentile city, *"each according to his ability*, decided to provide help" for their fellow believers by gathering together a special gift of money (Acts 11:29). Although we cannot argue conclusively that every Christian in Antioch participated, it seems that at least each family unit contributed what they could.

Some Christians, of course, cannot give anything—particularly during certain periods in their lives. For example, no one would expect the Christians in Jerusalem, who were suffering because of the famine, to give to others when they did not even have enough to meet their own needs. However, the time would come when they could reciprocate and meet the needs of other Christians (2 Corinthians 8:14).

Generally speaking, then, *all Christians can and should participate in using their material possessions to carry on God's work* (SCP 52). We must remember the example of some New Testament Christians who actually gave out of their poverty (2 Corinthians 8:2). Though their gifts may have been similar to that of the poor widow's gift, in God's sight it represented incredible generosity. Christians, therefore, must not hesitate to give just because they can only give a little.

2. GIVING REGULARLY, SYSTEMATICALLY, AND PROPORTIONATELY

When Paul wrote to the Corinthians, he exhorted them to put aside money in keeping with their income, saving it for when he came to pick it up. They were to do it regularly—on the first day of every week (1 Corinthians 16:2). Sometime earlier Paul had shared a special need with the Corinthians: a number of Christians in Jerusalem needed financial assistance. The Corinthians' initial response was positive and even enthusiastic (2 Corinthians 8:10-11). However, they had not followed through on their commitment.

They had failed to set aside money on a regular and systematic basis so that they would be prepared when Paul came to take their gift to Jerusalem. Consequently, Paul laid out a direct and specific plan. Following the tradition that quickly evolved in the first century, the Corinthian Christians were meeting on the first day of the week. Therefore, Paul exhorted every Christian in Corinth to "set aside a sum of money" on this day for this special offering.

With this injunction, Paul set forth an important principle: *Christians should set aside a certain percentage of their income on as regular a basis as they are paid to enable them to systematically give to God's work* (SCP 68). In both the Old and New Testaments, God teaches that giving should be systematic and regular. We are to be consistent in this area of our lives, just as in other areas of Christian living.

This focuses an important question. What percentage should a Christian set aside on a consistent basis from his regular income? The Holy Spirit did not lead New Testament writers to reiterate and perpetuate the Old Testament pattern involving specific amounts and percentages. But even though Christians are not obligated to follow the three-tithe system (see chapter 4, section 3), what the Israelites practiced at God's command provides believers with a strong pragmatic model for evaluating their own giving patterns:

First, if we are going to give systematically and regularly, we must decide to predetermine the percentage of our income or the fixed amount.

Second, if we are going to give "according to our ability" (as the Christians in Antioch did) and if we are going to give "proportionately" (as Paul exhorted the Corinthians to do), we must carefully and honestly determine how much that will be.

Third, if we are going to make sure God's work gets done in God's way, we must also look at the pragmatic factors involved: Why did God specify certain amounts to carry on His work in the Old Testament? Is there something unique about the 10 percent amount as it relates to supporting those who carry out the Great Commission on a full-time basis? Is there something special about the 10 percent amount to make sure family members worship God and learn His will as they should? Is there a practical reason for the 10 percent amount to be given every third year to help meet the needs of others not as fortunate as we are?

These are questions we must carefully consider when we determine how much we should give on a regular, systematic, and proportional basis. From a pragmatic perspective, one thing is crystal clear: If Christians gave the same amounts to the church as the Jews gave to maintain their religious system, there would never be unmet economic needs in the ministry. We could support Christian workers as never before, we could build church buildings debt free to minister to our families, and we could care for those who have serious financial needs. If all Christians, particularly in affluent cultures, gave proportionately as God has blessed them, some would be giving much more than three tithes to God's work.

3. RESPONDING IMMEDIATELY

The Corinthians had difficulty raising the amount of money they had originally hoped to give to the needy Christians in Jerusalem. Perhaps they were overly enthusiastic and unrealistic as to what they could do. Or they may have become victims of certain circumstances that made it difficult for them to follow through. However, Paul felt they had also been negligent in setting aside the monies on a week-to-week basis, which in turn meant they had not been carrying out this project regularly and systematically. Consequently, they were unable to reach their goal because they had already spent the money for their own needs and desires.

Paul recognized this problem. He knew that they would not be able to collect money they had already spent. He also recognized that because of this negligence on their part, they would not be able to give what they had hoped and originally planned to give. Therefore, he reminded them that what they set aside was "acceptable according to what they had" at that point in time (2 Corinthians 8:12). It would not, and should not, be evaluated on the basis of what they did *not* have.

The facts seem to be that if the Corinthians had tried to give as they had originally intended, it would have put them under unusual pressure. Money spent is money spent. Therefore, Paul encouraged them to begin where they were at that moment in their lives and to collect the money week by week on the basis of what they could do. God would then recognize and honor their "willingness." Paul put it this way: "For if the willingness is there, the gift is acceptable according to what one has, not according to what he does not have" (2 Corinthians 8:12).

This illustration in Scripture teaches us that *God accepts and honors our gifts once we begin to give regularly and systematically, even though we may not be able to give as proportionately as we eventually will be able to once we have our economic lives in order* (SCP 74). God wants all of us to begin immediately to organize our financial affairs so that we can put God first in the way we use our material possessions. We will see, however, that once we take this step, God often makes it possible for us to begin giving proportionately and in a generous way.

4. Making Faith Promises

The Corinthians made a promise based on projected future earnings. Thus, Paul wrote, "I thought it necessary to urge the brothers to visit you in advance to finish the arrangements for *the generous gift you had promised*" (2 Corinthians 9:5*a*). When the Corinthians made this promise, they were not presuming on God's grace. Otherwise, Paul would have admonished them for making a promise they could not fulfill. Conversely, he boasted to others about what they had planned to do. The Corinthian problem was not their promise but their failure to follow through on their commitment by setting aside money week by week from their earnings.

Paul set forth an important principle in terms of our stewardship: *God wants us to take a step of faith and trust Him to be able to give certain amounts of money based upon our future earnings* (SCP 79). If Christians only gave from what they had already accumulated, much of God's work would go undone. Paul knew it would take a lot of money to meet the needs of the poor Christians in Jerusalem. He also knew that the amount needed could not be generated with a "one-time" offering. Consequently, he presented the need to the various churches, asking people to make a long-range commitment and begin laying aside monies every week to fulfill their faith promise.

There are, of course, some common sense rules that must be applied in this kind of financial planning. First, we must project what we believe we can give based upon our potential performance, which must be evaluated realistically by both our past and present income. Most of us use this practical guideline regularly in terms of making purchases, planning business ventures, and working out budgets that cover many areas of our personal and vocational lives. Unfortunately, some Christians do not do this well and get themselves into serious financial difficulties.

The second guideline relates to the principle of faith. God wants us to trust Him for the future. He certainly does not want us to be unrealistic and foolish in our projections. But neither does He want us to be so reserved and hesitant that we do not trust Him to provide beyond what may be a human possibility. It takes wisdom, advice, and prayer to maintain a proper balance between proper planning and trusting God to provide.

5. GIVING WILLINGLY

When writing to the Corinthians, Paul made clear that *Christians should organize and plan their giving in a systematic way so that they could give generously, willingly, and joyfully, not in a grudging fashion* (2 Corinthians 9:5b; SCP 80). When money is available because we have planned our giving, it becomes a willing and joyful experience to share that money with others. We have not only prepared our hearts for "that moment," but we have prepared our hearts "ahead of time." We have arranged our giving in relationship to our overall financial plans. In America we call this a "budget."

Conversely, when Christians do not plan their giving, they usually do not have money to give. All of us tend to allow our standard of living to rise to our present level of income. Then, when we are asked to give, either regularly to meet the ongoing needs of the ministry or to make special gifts for special needs, we respond grudgingly. This is understandable since we have already spent our excess on our own needs and desires or have laid the excess aside for ourselves.

Under these circumstances, negative emotions are predictable. Oftentimes we not only have no excess to give to God's work but we are worried that we will not have enough money to meet what we believe to be our needs. This kind of predicament generates critical attitudes. Selfishness and guilt often blend together and cause us to blame our negligence on someone else. These are often the people who accuse Christian leaders of always talking about money, when in reality it may be mentioned only infrequently.

As the Corinthians demonstrate, the problem is usually not God's or that of the leaders who are attempting to carry on God's work by generating the necessary resources. It is our problem for not becoming systematic planners and givers. That is why Paul encouraged the Corinthians to prepare ahead of time: "Then it will be ready as a generous gift, not as one grudgingly given" (2 Corinthians 9:5b).

6. AVOIDING EMBARRASSMENT

Paul was anticipating that some of the Macedonian believers would accompany him when he went on to Corinth to collect their gifts for the saints in Jerusalem. Since Paul had been bragging about the way the Corinthians had initially responded to his challenge to help the poor, he wanted to make sure that they were prepared. He did not want to embarrass them or himself: "If any Macedonians come with me and find you unprepared, we—not to say anything about you—would be *ashamed* of having been so confident" (2 Corinthians 9:3-4).

This biblical illustration teaches that *when we make commitments, we should be on guard against embarrassing our spiritual leaders, as well as ourselves, by being negligent in following through on our commitments* (SCP 78). This is a pragmatic principle. Even the great apostle Paul was subject to embarrassment when people let him down. Christian leaders feel the same emotions today.

Understandably there will be circumstances that make it impossible for Christians to give as they had hoped and planned and even promised. However, the Corinthians' lack of response was caused primarily by their own negligence. Such behavior among Christians today makes life difficult for their leaders. It should not happen among those who claim to follow Jesus Christ.

7. Planning Ahead for Emergency Giving

"Therefore, *as we have opportunity*, let us do good to all people, especially to those who belong to the family of believers" (Galatians 6:10). When Paul told the Galatians to do good as they had "opportunity," it seems he was exhorting these Christians to utilize their opportunities in the immediate present *and* to plan ahead so they could take advantage of unforeseen opportunities. Practically speaking, this means that *Christians should not only set aside money to give regularly to support first and foremost their local church ministries but should also set aside money in preparation to meet emergency needs* (SCP 62). Opportunities always come our way to support worthy causes. If we do not have money in escrow for God's work, it will not be possible to experience the joy that comes from giving when these unforeseen opportunities present themselves.

Some believers I know actually have a special account in their bank entitled "God's emergency fund." This represents money set aside regularly to draw on when valid opportunities come their way to give beyond their regular "tithes" and "offerings." Obviously, if we do not plan this kind of giving into our regular stewardship plan, we will miss the joy and blessings that would be ours if the money were available to give.

8. Being Accountable

When it comes to giving, many of us have good intentions. Like the Corinthians, we may respond enthusiastically when we hear about special needs. However, also like the Corinthians, it is easy to forget commitments.

Notice how many steps Paul took to make sure the Corinthians followed through on their financial commitments:

- First, he sent Titus to help them complete the project (2 Corinthians 8:6).
- Second, he wrote them a personal letter encouraging them to "finish the work" (2 Corinthians 8:10-11).
- Third, he sent a group of "brothers" ahead of time to make sure they had collected the money before he himself had arrived (2 Corinthians 9:3).
- Fourth, he alerted them to his personal plans to arrive with some Macedonian Christians so that they would be prepared and not be embarrassed (2 Corinthians 9:4).

Paul's plan illustrates accountability. It also demonstrates how easy it is to conveniently forget what we have set out to do, especially when our own "desires" overshadow the "needs" of others. Consequently, we, too, need constant reminders. *We need to be held accountable when we make financial commitments to God's work* (SCP 71).

9. Giving What We Have

Dorcas, the woman Peter raised from the dead in Joppa, illustrates another important stewardship principle (Acts 9:32-43). *God desires to use Christians who may not have an abundance of material possessions but who unselfishly use what they have—including their skills—to do the work of God* (SCP 48). Though Dorcas was not well-to-do, she was skilled in making clothes, and she used that skill in helping others who were in need. Luke made sure he gave her story unusual prominence in the book of Acts.

And so it is today. God wants Christians involved in serving Jesus Christ with the resources at their disposal—though they may not have much when they compare themselves to others. The fact is, God does not want Christians to compare themselves to others in this sense. He wants all of us to be faithful with what we have.

10. Supporting Ourselves in Personal Ministries

The Scriptures contain dynamic examples of people with material resources who gave great segments of their time to the ministry while still providing for their personal and family needs. Philip was evidently this kind of man. He had a home and probably a business in Caesarea (Acts 21:8-9). However, he spent a great deal of time in missionary work, probably traveling at his own expense.

Aquila and Priscilla stand out as a rare example of a husband/wife team who supported themselves in ministry. They had been forced to leave Rome when the Emperor Claudius issued an order that all the Jews were to leave the city (Acts 18:1-2). They were tent makers by trade, a skill Paul had also developed. In the initial days of his ministry in Corinth, he made his living by using this skill, and in some way not described in Scripture he joined with Priscilla and Aquila in making tents (Acts 18:3).

It appears that Priscilla and Aquila became Christians at this time, probably after listening to their newly discovered business partner explain and interpret the Old Testament prophecies regarding Jesus Christ. When Paul left Corinth, this husband and wife team accompanied him until they reached Ephesus (Acts 18:19). They remained in Ephesus and continued the ministry while Paul continued on to his home church in Antioch (Acts 18:21-22, 26).

At some point in time, after the ban on Jews living in Rome was lifted, this dedicated couple left Ephesus and went back to their home in the imperial city. In his letter to the Roman Christians, Paul identified Aquila and Priscilla as his "fellow workers in Christ Jesus." In fact, he stated that "they risked their lives" for him (Romans 16:3-4). Obviously, they loved Jesus Christ, they loved Paul, and they loved the work of God. And when Paul greeted them following their return to Rome, they had once again opened their home as a meeting place for Christians (Romans 16:5*a*).

God needs people who can devote their full time to the ministry and be supported financially by those to whom they minister. But God also wants more men and women like Aquila and Priscilla. Following the model of New Testament Christians, *God desires to use people who are willing to utilize their own material resources to support themselves while they give great segments of their time to the ministry* (SCP 47).

The affluence in many parts of our own society today is making this possible as in no other moment in history. I have personally challenged people to plan their retirement so that they can support themselves in ministry, actually traveling to various parts of the world to do missionary work. One couple I know is actually planning early retirement to achieve this goal. What an incredible way to spend the most mature years of our lives serving Jesus Christ.

Note that the Scriptures do not teach that we should save money to support ourselves at some future time *instead of* giving to support present ministries. That would violate other biblical principles. Saving funds for a future personal ministry is simply one additional way affluent Christians can plan to utilize their excess income in creative ways in order to build the kingdom of God and to store up treasures in heaven.

11. Supporting Our Local Church

The local church should be God's primary context for both systematic giving and maintaining accountability in the area of material possessions (SCP 16, 87). Paul affirmed and expanded on these two interrelated principles in his second letter to the Corinthians:

- First, he was writing to the *local* church at Corinth (8:10).
- Second, he began his discourse on giving by using the Macedonian *churches* as a model (8:1).
- Third, when he informed the Corinthians that he was going to be sending along another "brother," he made sure they knew that this man was "praised by all the *churches*" and "chosen by the *churches*" to accompany Paul, Titus, and the offering to Jerusalem (8:18-19). That is why Paul could say that these men were "representatives of the *churches*" (9:23).

Practically speaking, there is no feasible way for individual Christians to be held accountable when they are not participating members of a local body of believers. God designed churches to be this kind of accountability system in all areas of our Christian lives—including the way we give. Christians who purposely avoid being accountable to other believers and to their spiritual leaders are just as guilty of being unsubmissive to the will of God as are Christian leaders who refuse to make themselves accountable to other members of the Body of Christ.

Does the Bible teach, then, that Christians should give only to their local churches in order to practice the principle of accountability? No. However, Christians should evaluate their giving patterns to organizations outside their own local churches by considering other important guidelines that God gives in Scripture.

- To what extent are we supporting those who are ministering to us and to our families?
- What percentage of our income are we actually giving to our local church? Though certainly not an absolute guideline, a good rule of thumb is for Christians to set a goal to give at least 10 percent of their income to their local churches before they support additional ministries. God's plan in the Old Testament required the Israelites to give 10 percent to support their spiritual leaders. If we use this approach as a pragmatic example, it will guarantee that local church leaders and ministries will never be neglected by the people they are ministering to.
- What kind of accountability system does the parachurch organization promote and practice?
- What kind of reputation does the parachurch organization and its leaders have in their Christian community, as well as in the world at large?

Paul was concerned about accountability. "We want to avoid any criticism by the way we administer this liberal gift. For we are taking pains to do what is right, not only in the eyes of the Lord but also in the eyes of men" (2 Corinthians 8:20).

12. Recognizing Our Obligations

When Paul wrote to the Romans, he was preparing to leave for Jerusalem with a group of men to deliver the gift of money for needy Christians. In fact, he reported that he was already on his way (Romans 15:25), which probably meant that he was ready to leave for Jerusalem the moment he finished his dictation. The money that had been collected over a period of time by the churches in Macedonia and Achaia was in hand (1 Corinthians 16:1-5).

As Paul began to conclude this letter, he explained the spirit and motivation that caused these Macedonian and Achaian Christians to gather this money. First, "they were *pleased* to do it" (Romans 15:27*a*). In spite of the problems that had occurred in Corinth, Paul could now share the concern and compassion these Christians demonstrated toward the Jewish Christians in Jerusalem who were suffering from economic deprivation. Evidently the Corinthians had responded maturely to Paul's exhortations (2 Corinthians 8–9).

Paul went on to state *why* a Christian should share his material possessions with others. Though the churches in Macedonia and Achaia responded out of concern, Paul made clear that they also had an *obligation* to help the needy Christians in Jerusalem: "they owe it to them" (Romans 15:27*b*). Then he explained why: The message of Christianity came first to the Jews. Jesus Christ Himself was a Jew. The apostles were all Jews. The first converts to Christianity were Jews. And it was the Jewish Christians in Jerusalem who first brought the message of Jesus Christ to the Gentiles, primarily because of persecution (Acts 8:1, 4; Acts 11:19-21).

In Paul's letter to the Romans, then, we have another important principle: *All Christians have an obligation to support God's work in material ways* (SCP 91). Such a statement may raise a question in our minds. Earlier Paul clarified that God does not want Christians to respond to a *command* to share their material possessions but to respond out of hearts of love that reflect sincere appreciation for His gift of salvation in Christ (2 Corinthians 8:8-9). Furthermore, every Christian is ultimately responsible to give to God on the basis of his own heart decision (2 Corinthians 9:7).

It may appear that this third principle from Romans, therefore, contradicts other principles. But in reality, these principles are complementary not contradictory. To understand this apparent tension more fully, we need to consider a larger perspective on Christian commitment.

According to Scripture we are all obligated to present ourselves to God because of His gift of eternal salvation in Christ. At the same time, however, we should present our bodies to God freely in response to His mercy, love, and grace. Just so, we have an obligation to give to God's work. However, it should at the same time be given freely and voluntarily from hearts of love. In Christ, it is possible to blend these two concepts. Once we understand God's grace, it becomes a "blessed obligation" to give, not an "oppressive burden."

13. Avoiding Subjectivity in Giving

As we conclude this study on God's specific plan for giving, *we should recognize how important it is not to evaluate subjectively what we believe is the Holy Spirit's leading when it comes to giving* (SCP 36). This is not to deny that the Holy Spirit desires to lead every Christian in how they should use their material possessions to further the kingdom of God. However, we must not rely on "inner promptings" regarding our use of material blessings without making sure that those perceptions are in harmony with God's revealed truth in the Scriptures. We need to evaluate internal impressions and inner thoughts with the objective principles of the written Word of God.

This is true in all areas of life, but particularly important in the area of giving. Since material things can become so intricately related to "who we are as human beings," as well as to our natural tendencies to be self-oriented, our "inner promptings" may be primarily selfish. It is easy to rationalize in this area of our Christian lives and to deceive ourselves. We need the objective truth of the Word of God to evaluate whether or not we are in the will of God. This is particularly important in determining how much we give, when we give, and where and to whom we give. And most basic, we must evaluate our motives in the light of the Scriptures: the why of our giving. Hopefully, the principles outlined in this chapter will help all of us to be obedient to the Word of God and to avoid our natural tendencies to "love ourselves" more than we love God and others.

Let's Check Ourselves

On a scale of one to ten, circle the number that best represents how well you believe the people in your church or group practice the biblical principle found in each question.

1. Are the believers in our church involved in sharing what they have to help others in need?

VERY LITTLE				SOMEWHAT				EXTENSIVELY	
1	2	3	4	5	6	7	8	9	10

2. Do the believers in our church set aside a portion of every paycheck to be given to the Lord's work on a regular, systematic, and proportional basis?

VERY LITTLE				SOMEWHAT				EXTENSIVELY	
1	2	3	4	5	6	7	8	9	1 0

3. Do the believers in the church understand that, once they begin to give regularly and systematically, God honors their gifts based upon their willingness to give at that moment in their lives?

VERY LITTLE				SOMEWHAT				EXTENSIVELY	
1	2	3	4	5	6	7	8	9	1 0

4. Do the Christians in our church include God in their financial planning, trusting Him to make it possible through future earnings to give regularly, systematically, and proportionately?

VERY LITTLE				SOMEWHAT				EXTENSIVELY	
1	2	3	4	5	6	7	8	9	1 0

5. Do the Christians in our church give willingly and joyfully because the money is available through careful and systematic planning?

VERY LITTLE				SOMEWHAT				EXTENSIVELY	
1	2	3	4	5	6	7	8	9	1 0

6. Do the people in our church maintain their financial commitments to the Lord so as not to be an embarrassment to themselves or to our leaders?

VERY LITTLE				SOMEWHAT				EXTENSIVELY	
1	2	3	4	5	6	7	8	9	1 0

7. Do people in our church plan their giving so that they not only give regularly, systematically, and proportionately but also have funds set aside to meet emergency needs in carrying out God's work?

VERY LITTLE				SOMEWHAT				EXTENSIVELY	
1	2	3	4	5	6	7	8	9	1 0

8. Are believers in our church held accountable when they make financial commitments to God's work?

VERY LITTLE				SOMEWHAT				EXTENSIVELY	
1	2	3	4	5	6	7	8	9	1 0

9. Do people in our church who have very little of this world's goods use their talents and abilities to serve others?

VERY LITTLE				SOMEWHAT				EXTENSIVELY	
1	2	3	4	5	6	7	8	9	10

10. Do people in our church who are relatively well-to-do use their resources to enable them to devote large segments of time to the ministry?

VERY LITTLE				SOMEWHAT				EXTENSIVELY	
1	2	3	4	5	6	7	8	9	10

11. Do the people in our church realize that one reason God ordained the local church is so that they can be assured that the money they give is used in a responsible and God-honoring way and so that they can be held accountable?

VERY LITTLE				SOMEWHAT				EXTENSIVELY	
1	2	3	4	5	6	7	8	9	10

12. Do the Christians in our church realize that they have an obligation to give to God's work, even though God wants us to give out of willing and joyful hearts?

VERY LITTLE				SOMEWHAT				EXTENSIVELY	
1	2	3	4	5	6	7	8	9	10

13. Are the people in our church planning and practicing their giving based on the objective principles of Scripture rather than on subjective feelings?

VERY LITTLE				SOMEWHAT				EXTENSIVELY	
1	2	3	4	5	6	7	8	9	10

How to Use This Evaluation Exercise

1. Duplicate these thirteen questions on a separate sheet, and have each person in your group anonymously evaluate your church.
2. Tabulate the responses to find an average score. To do so, total the numbers circled in each question. Divide this total number by the number of people responding to that particular question. This will give you a "mean," or average, score.

3. Discover the greatest needs in your church by arranging the scores numerically from the highest to the lowest. Those scores that are lowest represent the areas that need immediate attention.

4. In discussing these scores and the principles involved, spend time first of all reviewing the areas of strength in your church. Spend time in prayer, thanking God for those strengths.

5. Finally, spend time discussing ways to practice the principles that are the most neglected in your church. The following questions will help:

   a. What are the areas of greatest need?

   b. What can we do that we are not doing to practice these biblical principles?

   c. What specific goals can we set up to practice these principles?

   d. What can we do *immediately*?

PERSONALIZE THIS PROJECT

Follow the procedure described at the end of chapter 1.

12

Christians and Debt

As in all free enterprise systems, the economy of the New Testament world was highly integrated with financial dealings that involved indebtedness. However, neither Jesus Christ nor the New Testament writers addressed this subject in a direct fashion. Jesus simply acknowledged the practice of borrowing and loaning money in the Roman Empire without making value judgments on these practices per se. He often used these economic settings as illustrative material to teach spiritual truths (see chapter 2, section 2).

Why, then, deal with the issue? Even though Jesus and the apostles did not address the subject of debt directly, many New Testament principles dealing with our material possessions do relate to this subject. Furthermore, the Old Testament contains a number of statements about debt. It is important that we understand these teachings and integrate them with New Testament principles.

1. PAYING WHAT WE OWE

The text that is most frequently referred to in relationship to debt is found in Paul's letter to the Romans: "Let no debt remain outstanding, except the continuing debt to love one another, for he who loves his fellowman has fulfilled the law" (Romans 13:8).

A casual reading of this exhortation may give the impression that Paul was teaching that it is always wrong to borrow money. Most serious commentators disagree with such an understanding of Paul's teaching. John Murray is representative when he says "This cannot be taken to mean that we may never issue financial obligations, that we may not borrow from others in case of need."[1]

It may be unwise and even out of God's will to borrow money in certain circumstances, but that is not what Paul was referring to in this verse. He was simply saying that if we owe money, we should pay it. In context, this includes taxes and every kind of revenue that is required by the government (Romans 13:7).

The Scriptures broaden this concept to include *any kind of debt.* In the New Testament world it involved wages. That is why James wrote "Look! The wages you failed to pay the workmen who mowed your fields are crying out against you. The cries of the harvesters have reached the ears of the Lord Almighty" (James 5:4). It is utterly sinful to hire people to perform tasks and then not to pay them.

In addition, Paul's command certainly includes the repayment of any money that has been borrowed. And it goes without saying that there should be repayment of anything that has ever been stolen. Paul was so conscientious about this kind of obligation that after he led Onesimus to Christ, he personally offered to repay Philemon (Onesimus's owner) anything this slave had stolen (Philemon 17).

In essence, Paul was teaching that *Christians who owe people money or goods to always pay what they owe* (SCP 90). It is indeed unfortunate that some who claim to be followers of Jesus Christ violate this principle with every degree of regularity. Some Christians simply borrow money and do not repay it. Or if they do make payments, they are always late or woefully behind.

This kind of behavior is even more deplorable when it characterizes pastors and other Christian leaders. I have heard tragic stories of ministers who have transferred to churches in other cities, leaving behind a string of unpaid debts. Fortunately, these situations seem to be the exception rather than the rule. But even a single instance among those who claim to be spiritual leaders is one too many.

THE OLD TESTAMENT SETTING

A. E. Willingale gives us some helpful insights concerning the cultural, economic, and spiritual differences that existed in Israel prior to the time they went into captivity and before they eventually became a part of the Roman Empire. Speaking of the time that Israel occupied the Promised Land and determined her own economic destiny, he states,

> Loans in Israel were not commercial but charitable, granted not to enable a trader to set up or expand a business but to tide a peasant farmer over a period of poverty. Since the economy remained predominately agricultural up to the end of the monarchy, there developed no counterpart to the commercial loan system already existing in Babylonia in 2000 B.C. Hence the legislation contains not mercantile regulations but exhortations to neighbourliness.[2]

These facts provide the necessary backdrop for interpreting the Old Testament passages regarding debt. In the first place, there was no need for

Israelites to purchase property since they had received it at no cost from God Himself (Deuteronomy 6:10b-11). And, because of God's material provisions for the children of Israel, there was no need to establish businesses based upon a free enterprise system. Rather, they were able to make a living from the land they had received free from indebtedness. Initially, at least, they did not even need to build houses and plant the fields (Deuteronomy 6:10-12). Consequently, business loans of any kind were unnecessary.

God had also promised His people that He would provide unusual spiritual *and* material blessings if they obeyed Him: "The Lord will open the heavens, the storehouse of his bounty, to send rain on your land in season and to bless all the work of your hands. *You will lend to many nations but will borrow from none*" (Deuteronomy 28:12-13).

THE NEW TESTAMENT SETTING

This unique economic setting in Israel changed in the New Testament. Israel now existed in a totally different cultural and economic environment. The Jews had to adapt their laws to a commercial economy. In some instances, they circumvented some of these laws for purely selfish reasons. On the other hand, they could not practice some of the laws and survive in Roman culture. Jesus recognized this reality in that He did not address these issues directly.

THE TWENTIETH-CENTURY SETTING

The challenge we face as twentieth-century Christians is to interpret the Old Testament teachings regarding borrowing and debt without transplanting Old Testament laws into another cultural setting in a legalistic, literal fashion. At the same time, we must not bypass the spirit of these laws. Though designed for Israel, they yield timeless principles that are affirmed in the New Testament. We will look at the major Old Testament teachings with this challenge in mind.

2. LENDING TO HELP OTHERS IN NEED

When speaking to the issue of lending money, God gave the following law: "If you lend money to any of my people among you who is needy, do not be like a moneylender; charge him no interest" (Exodus 22:25).

When the children of Israel came into Canaan, God gave them everything, with the promise that, if they obeyed Him, He would give them even more. However, the Lord stated that there would "always be poor people" among them (Deuteronomy 15:11). Thus, He prefaced this law on lending money free of interest in Exodus 22:25 by warning the Israelites to never "take advantage of a widow or an orphan. If you do, and they cry out to me, I will certainly hear their cry. My anger will be aroused, and I will kill you with a sword; your wives will become widows and your children fatherless" (Exodus 22:22-24).

The picture is clear. How could those who had received all these material possessions as a free gift from God turn around and take advantage of the poor and needy? How could they even consider loaning money and charging interest to their fellow Israelites who were already in a desperate financial plight? To do so would be an ultimate act of selfishness and sin. (Also see Exodus 22:26-27; Leviticus 25:35-38).

What is the principle in this Old Testament law that is binding on Christians today? Is God saying that it is always wrong to charge a fellow believer interest on money that we lend to them? The answer must be "no." We are living in a cultural setting quite different from Israel. However, if a Christian in *any cultural situation* ever takes advantage of another Christian—especially poor people—there is no question that it is sinful and selfish behavior. It is an affront to God who has freely given us the gift of salvation, as well as material blessings.

The principle, then, can be stated as follows: *Christians must never take economic advantage of poor people, whether they be Christians or non-Christians* (SCP 92). This truth is validated throughout the Word of God.

3. Experiencing God's Blessings

Reflecting on God's promises to Israel regarding the Promised Land, David once wrote: "The wicked borrow and do not repay, but the righteous give generously" (Psalm 37:21). In essence, David was saying that if the Israelites obeyed the Lord in all respects, it would never be necessary for them to borrow money from their pagan neighbors. They would always have sufficient for themselves and plenty left over to give to others. Conversely, wicked people—those who do not obey the laws of God—will find themselves in a state of desperation. They will have to borrow money to survive and never have enough resources to pay it back.

Inherent in David's parable is a profound principle affirmed in the New Testament: *Christians who obey God's Word will be able not only to meet their own economic needs but the needs of others as well* (SCP 93) Though certain literal aspects of God's promises to Israel as a nation are not applicable to Christians today, other aspects are. The New Testament affirms that God will meet our needs if we are righteous and generous people (see SCP 83, 84).

4. Showing Mercy to Others in Crises

In the book of Deuteronomy, the Lord gave certain commands to the Israelites regarding the cancelling of debts:

At the end of every seven years you must *cancel debts.* This is how it is to be done: Every creditor shall cancel the loan he has made to his fellow Israelite. He shall not require payment from his fellow Israelite or brother, because the Lord's time for canceling debts has been proclaimed. You may require payment from a foreigner, but you must cancel any debt your brother owes you. (Deuteronomy 15:1-3)

Two important factors need to be considered in explaining what God had in mind with this law.

First, note once again the context of this commandment. Moses had just reminded the people of their responsibility to "the aliens, the fatherless and the widows" who lived among them. "At the end of *every three years,*" they were to "bring all the tithes of that year's produce and store it in" the various towns. Then, those in need could "come and eat and be satisfied" (Deuteronomy 14:28-29). Moses next went on to state their responsibility "at the end of *every seven years*" (Deuteronomy 15:1) toward poor people who had borrowed money just to survive. Moses was outlining laws that were to govern relationships with people who were economically desperate.

Second, note what Moses was actually saying in a still larger context. In the book of Exodus, God had commanded the people of Israel to sow their fields and harvest their crops for six years. However, "during the seventh year," they were to "let the land lie unplowed and unused. Then, the poor among your people may get food from it, and the wild animals may eat what they leave. Do the same with your vineyard and your olive grove" (Exodus 23:10-11).

The command to cancel debts relates to this seven-year period of time (Deuteronomy 15:1-3). God was expressing concern for the poor people who had borrowed money from their fellow Israelites. They, too, were not allowed to cultivate their fields during the seventh year. Keil and Delitzsch explain: "If no harvest was gathered in, and even such produce as had grown without sowing was to be left to the poor and the beasts of the field, the landowner could have no income from which to pay his debts."[3]

Consequently, Moses outlined a plan for handling these debts. Those who had loaned money to poor people, which was to be loaned without interest (Exodus 22:25), were not to put pressure on them to pay back what they owed during this seventh year. Keil and Delitzsch translate verse 2 as follows: "This is the manner of the release. Every owner of a loan of his hand shall release [leave] what he has lent to his neighbour; he shall not press his neighbour, and indeed his brother; for they have proclaimed release for Jehovah."

Moses was not issuing a command to cancel debts once and for all as some have supposed. Rather, debt payments were simply to be postponed during this seventh year. Relative to what God had in mind, Wilhelm J.

Schroeder adds this helpful comment: "It seems further clear that the release had reference only to loans, and to *loans lent because of poverty*, not to debts contracted in the purchase of goods."[4]

Since the command to cancel debts relates to Israel's agricultural economy and God's special arrangements for His people in the Promised Land, what, then, is the principle for us today? Interpreted in the light of New Testament teachings, it seems clear that *Christians must set the example of being gracious to people who have borrowed money with good intentions and then have faced crises beyond their control that have made it difficult for them to make their loan payments on time* (SCP 94).

This principle raises some practical questions. Since there will always be times when people borrow money and have difficulty repaying it, what should we do? If we have made a personal loan to a fellow Christian, we naturally have more control over the circumstances. Furthermore, these loans should be made with full awareness that those we are attempting to help may not be able to repay. In other words, we should be willing to make the loan a gift if necessary or to postpone payments indefinitely. This decision should be made in our hearts and minds before we ever make personal loans to a brother or sister in Christ. This does not mean, however, that any Christian who borrows from another Christian should purposely take advantage of their graciousness and neglect to repay the loan in a responsible manner.

Is it right for a Christian to ever make a loan to a fellow Christian and charge interest? The Scriptures do not speak to this question when it relates to business ventures in a culture that is based on a free enterprise system. However, the overall teachings of the Bible do make clear that *to loan money to poor people with the intent of making money violates both Old and New Testament principles* (SCP 92).

5. CAREFULLY EVALUATING ALL RISKS

One powerful Proverb says, "The rich rule over the poor, and the borrower is servant to the lender" (Proverbs 22:7). A dramatic event that helps us understand this Proverb took place after a number of Israelites returned to the Promised Land from captivity under the leadership of Zerubbabel (536 B.C.) and then under Ezra (458 B.C.).

Several years later when Nehemiah arrived to help rebuild the walls of Jerusalem, he found an incredible situation. Because of a famine, many of the poor people in Israel had already mortgaged their fields, their vineyards, and their homes to buy grain (Nehemiah 5:3). Still others, to keep their property, had borrowed money from their Jewish brothers to pay taxes to King Artaxerxes (Nehemiah 5:4). The problem was compounded by the fact that these fellow Jews charged these poor people interest, which, of course, was a direct violation of the laws of Moses. To add insult to injury, they charged exorbitant rates.

Those who borrowed money to survive faced yet another crisis when their crops failed. Because of the famine, their Jewish brothers and sisters took away their property and sold their children into slavery. Thus, the people cried out to Nehemiah.

> Although we are of the same flesh and blood as our countrymen and though our sons are as good as theirs, yet we have to subject our sons and daughters to slavery. Some of our daughters have already been enslaved, but we are powerless, because our fields and our vineyards belong to others. (Nehemiah 5:5)

Solomon's Proverb is literally illustrated in this situation.

Nehemiah confronted this situation directly. He rebuked the nobles and officials among the Jews. "I told them, 'You are exacting usury [interest] from your own countrymen!'" (Nehemiah 5:7*b*). Nehemiah was so disturbed that he called a large meeting to deal with the problem.

> What you are doing is not right. Shouldn't you walk in the fear of our God to avoid the reproach of our Gentile enemies? I and my brothers and my men are also lending the people money and grain. But let the exacting of usury [interest] stop! Give back to them immediately their fields, vineyards, olive groves and houses, and also the usury you are charging them—the hundredth part of the money, grain, new wine and oil. (Nehemiah 5:9-11)

Fortunately, the Israelites responded to Nehemiah's exhortations. Had they not done so, God's judgment would have fallen on them, as it had before, because of their selfish and greedy behavior.

Solomon in all his wisdom understood this kind of social disease and sin. His words were directed more specifically to the rich than to the poor, for it was they who had the power to "rule over the poor." It is the rich who force "the borrower" to be "servant to the lender." It is they who exploit these innocent people at will, particularly in times of economic deprivation.

What is the principle that Christians need to learn from this Old Testament Proverb? We must realize that any form of borrowing brings with it a certain amount of bondage. As Otto Zockler asserts, "indebtedness always destroys freedom, even though no sale into slavery of him who is unable to pay should ever take place."[5] This observation, of course, does not mean that borrowing per se is wrong. However, it does teach that, *before we borrow money for any purpose, we should consider all the circumstances and seek wisdom from others who can help us evaluate all aspects of the decision, including the risks involved* (SCP 95). The lower the risk, the less the sense of bondage.

In conclusion, we might ask ourselves this important question: What will we actually lose if we cannot repay the loan? For example, could we possibly be obligated the rest of our lives? That is a terrible price to pay for attempting to achieve an economic goal. In that sense, Solomon's statement is very applicable. Economically, we become "slaves."

6. Being Cautious Regarding Cosignatures

On several occasions, the Scriptures warn against securing a loan for someone else. "Do not be a man who strikes hands in pledge or puts up security for debts; if you lack the means to pay, your very bed will be snatched from under you" (Proverbs 22:26-27). A careful look at this exhortation in context, and others like it (Proverbs 6:1, 5; 11:15; 17:18), reveals that Solomon's exhortations are not in themselves making judgments on those who are "lenders." Rather, he is warning those who might become victims. Those who often put up surety were also poor, for if they were not, they could have easily covered the debt involved.

Some interpret these passages to indicate that it is out of the will of God to ever "put up security" for another person. But A. R. Fausset says, "This precept does not forbid suretiship in cases where charity and brotherly kindness dictate it." Rather, he believes that Solomon's teaching "only forbids such suretiship as is without a due regard to one's self, to him for whom you are surety, and to the other party to whom you make yourself bound."[6]

Applied to our lives today, it appears that there are times when a Christian may cosign a note for another individual without violating the will of God. In fact, it may be a gracious and generous act of love. However, *Christians who decide to guarantee a loan in this way should be willing and able to cover the complete debt in case of default without serious consequences to themselves, their families, or the Lord's work* (SCP 96).

Another word of caution is in order before leaving this subject. Even in our culture today, it is wise to generalize these Old Testament warnings against cosigning notes and to encourage others who need help to wait until they are in such a financial position so as not to need this kind of economic assistance. Though there are exceptions to this rule, they should be made rarely and cautiously, considering all the scriptural principles that relate to how a Christian should view and use his material possessions.

7. Borrowing According to Biblical Principles

If the Scriptures do not teach against borrowing per se, then when does going into debt become an irresponsible decision that leads us directly out of the will of God and into sinful attitudes and actions? To answer this question, we must refer back to Paul's statement in the book of Romans to "let no debt remain outstanding" (Romans 13:8*a*). As stated earlier, all borrowing involves a certain amount of risk. But when we make foolish decisions based upon ignorance, we are acting irresponsibly and can quickly find ourselves in violation of God's will. Furthermore, *if we ever knowingly borrow money that we cannot pay back according to a predetermined agreement, we are at that moment guilty of both lying and stealing* (SCP 97).

Several guidelines will help us to avoid irresponsible decisions that lead us to sin against God:

• We are out of God's will when we borrow money to buy things to glorify ourselves and not God (Matthew 6:3-4).

• We are out of God's will when we borrow because we are in bondage to materialism (Matthew 6:24), when our treasures are on earth rather than in heaven.

• We are out of God's will when any form of dishonesty is involved in borrowing money (1 Timothy 6:10).

• We are out of God's will when we use borrowed money to achieve any goals that are out of the will of God (Romans 12:1-2).

8. Putting God First in Our Financial Planning

There is another important principle that grows out of all we have learned thus far in this study that will help us know if we are out of the will of God when we borrow money. Unfortunately, many Christians in American culture are violating this principle with every degree of regularity. Succinctly stated, when we cannot set aside money on a regular, systematic, and proportional basis for God's work because we have obligated ourselves financially, we have ceased putting God first in our lives. Put another way, *Christians are out of God's will when they cannot give God the "firstfruits" of their income because they have obligated themselves to pay off debts* (1 Corinthians 16:2; SCP 98).

This certainly would not be true, of course, in some instances, when we experience economic reversals beyond our control. In most cases, however, being unable to put God first happens when we have materialistic goals which, in turn, lead us to make irresponsible decisions. We should never borrow money that knowingly makes it impossible, even temporarily, to give to God's work regularly, systematically, and proportionately. How do we correct this problem if we are out of the will of God in this area of our lives?

First, we should confess our sins to God and accept His forgiveness (1 John 1:9).

Second, we must take steps as quickly as possible to bring our lives into harmony with God's will. If we owe money we cannot pay, we need to immediately draw up a plan to correct the situation.

Third, we must include in this plan a way to give regularly and systematically to God's work.

This third point poses another question. Should Christians give regularly and systematically to the Lord's work when they have debt payments that are overdue? In answering this question, Larry Burkett gives a helpful suggestion. He believes that "the first portion of everything we receive belongs to God. It doesn't belong to anybody else, even a creditor." Furthermore, he points out that Christians who make a commitment to give regularly to God are "always better money handlers, and as a result of their commitment to God, they will honor their commitment to their creditors." It has also been his experience that "rarely does a creditor object to this arrangement once he understands this kind of commitment."[7]

Burkett is advocating that Christians who are behind in debt payments should contact their creditors with a plan of action, spelling out how they are going to care for these debts on a regular and systematic basis. They should also include in their plan their intentions to give a certain amount of their income regularly and systematically to their church.

Burkett has experienced that most creditors feel comfortable with this kind of planning, since it indicates honesty and moral integrity. People who have these values can normally be trusted to pay off their debts over a period of time. Furthermore, Christians who establish these priorities will be honored and blessed by God in economic ways that will eventually enable them not only to meet their financial obligations to their creditors but also be able to begin to give to God's work, not only regularly and systematically, but proportionately as well.

NOTES

1. John Murray, *The New International Commentary on the New Testament: The Epistle to the Romans*, 2 vols. (Grand Rapids: Eerdmans, 1965), p. 158.

2. A. E. Willingale, *The New Bible Dictionary* (Grand Rapids: Eerdmans, 1962), p. 304.

3. C. F. Keil and F. Delitzsch, *The Pentateuch*, vol. 1 of *Commentary on the Old Testament in Ten Volumes*, trans. James Martin (Grand Rapids: Eerdmans, 1973), p. 370.

4. Wilhelm J. Schroeder, *Deuteronomy*, Lange's Commentary on the Holy Scriptures, vol. 2, trans. and ed. Philip Schaff (Grand Rapids: Zondervan, 1969), p. 136.

5. Otto Zockler, *The Proverbs of Solomon*, Lange's Commentary on the Holy Scriptures, vol. 5, p. 192.

6. A. R. Fausset, *A Commentary: Critical, Experimental and Practical on the Old and New Testaments*, vol. 3 (Grand Rapids: Eerdmans, 1948), p. 429.

7. Larry Burkett, *Answers to Your Family's Financial Questions* (Pomona, Calif.: Focus on the Family, 1987), pp. 112-13.

LET'S CHECK OURSELVES

On a scale of one to ten, circle the number that best represents how well you believe the people in your church or group practice the biblical principle found in each question.

1. Do people in our church pay money to those they owe money?

VERY LITTLE				SOMEWHAT				EXTENSIVELY	
1	2	3	4	5	6	7	8	9	10

2. Are people in our church taking advantage of poor people by lending them money for which they charge interest?

VERY LITTLE				SOMEWHAT				EXTENSIVELY	
1	2	3	4	5	6	7	8	9	10

3. Do the Christians in our church understand that, if they walk in the will of God, they will always be able to help meet the physical needs of those less fortunate than they are?

VERY LITTLE				SOMEWHAT				EXTENSIVELY	
1	2	3	4	5	6	7	8	9	10

4. Are the people in our church who have loaned money to others sensitive to their plight during times of crises that are beyond their control?

VERY LITTLE				SOMEWHAT				EXTENSIVELY	
1	2	3	4	5	6	7	8	9	10

5. Are believers in our church in debt because they have been influenced by a materialistic philosophy of life rather than by a biblical approach to both accumulating and sharing their material possessions?

VERY LITTLE				SOMEWHAT				EXTENSIVELY	
1	2	3	4	5	6	7	8	9	10

6. Do people in our church cosign notes that could lead them to personal financial disaster, possibly devastating their families and negatively affecting their relationships with other Christians, with unbelievers, and with God Himself?

VERY LITTLE				SOMEWHAT				EXTENSIVELY	
1	2	3	4	5	6	7	8	9	10

7. Are people in our church unable to make debt payments because of irresponsible borrowing?

VERY LITTLE				SOMEWHAT				EXTENSIVELY	
1	2	3	4	5	6	7	8	9	10

8. Are Christians in our church unable to give regularly, systematically, and proportionately because of their debts?

VERY LITTLE				SOMEWHAT				EXTENSIVELY	
1	2	3	4	5	6	7	8	9	10

How to Use This Evaluation Exercise

1. Duplicate these eight questions on a separate sheet, and have each person in your group anonymously evaluate your church.
2. Tabulate the responses to find an average score. To do so, total the numbers circled in each question. Divide this total number by the number of people responding to that particular question. This will give you a "mean," or average, score.
3. Discover the greatest needs in your church by arranging the scores numerically from the highest to the lowest. Those scores that are lowest represent the areas that need immediate attention.
4. In discussing these scores and the principles involved, spend time first of all reviewing the areas of strength in your church. Spend time in prayer, thanking God for those strengths.
5. Finally, spend time discussing ways to practice the principles that are the most neglected in your church. The following questions will help:
    a. What are the areas of greatest need?
    b. What can we do that we are not doing to practice these biblical principles?
    c. What specific goals can we set up to practice these principles?
    d. What can we do *immediately*?

Personalize This Project

Follow the procedure described at the end of chapter 1.

13

Giving and the Will of God

It may be startling for some Christians living in the midst of the twentieth-century world to realize that more is recorded in Scripture about material possessions and how Christians are to use them for the glory of God than any other aspect of Christian living—including principles for maintaining sexual purity. No aspect of life is more important in determining whether or not we are living in the perfect will of God.

1. REFLECTING THE WILL OF GOD

When the apostle Paul exhorted and pleaded with the Roman Christians to offer their bodies to Christ, he certainly had in mind how Christians are to use their material possessions. Paul affirmed this fact when he wrote to the Philippian Christians and thanked them for their gifts of money sent to sustain him in prison. Their *material gifts* to Paul were an extension of the *gift of themselves* to God.

Compare Paul's statement to the Romans with what he says to the Philippians:

Romans 12:1

"Therefore, I urge you, brothers, in view of God's mercy, to offer your bodies as living sacrifices, holy and pleasing to God—which is your spiritual worship."

Philippians 4:18

"I have received full payment and even more; I am amply supplied, now that I have received from Epaphroditus the gifts you sent. They are a fragrant offering, an acceptable sacrifice, pleasing to God."

These verses contain the following specific comparisons:

GIVING THEIR BODIES	GIVING THEIR MATERIAL GIFTS
Romans 12:1	Philippians 4:18
"Offer your bodies"	"The gifts you sent"
"Living sacrifices"	"An acceptable sacrifice"
"Pleasing to God"	"Pleasing to God"
"Your spiritual worship"	"A fragrant offering"

Writing to the Corinthians, Paul again underscored this correlation and sequence. He referred to the Christians in Macedonia (probably the Philippians or the Thessalonians) as models: "For I testify that they gave as much as they were able, and even beyond their ability. . . . They gave themselves first to the Lord and then to us [their material gifts] in keeping with God's will" (2 Corinthians 8:3-5).

Stated in terms of a principle, the Word of God teaches that *the way Christians use their material possessions is an important criterion for determining whether or not they are living in the will of God* (SCP 15). With few exceptions, it is not possible to be in the perfect will of God unless we are giving our "firstfruits" to God and doing so regularly, systematically, and proportionately. The exception to this conclusion would be that we have set this as our goal and we are prayerfully and diligently working toward that goal. In such a situation, Paul reminds us that "if the willingness is there, the gift is acceptable according to what one has, not according to what he does not have" (2 Corinthians 8:12).

2. Responding Immediately to God's Truth

When it comes to giving, *Christians should respond immediately to whatever portion of God's truth they have received* (SCP 17). This principle, of course, applies to all areas of a Christian's life, but it applies particularly to the way we view and use our material possessions. The believers in Jerusalem did not understand many aspects of what would eventually emerge as a more stabilized economic situation. Initially they were expecting Jesus Christ to return to "restore the kingdom to Israel" (Acts 1:6), even though Christ had made clear that it was not for them "to know the times or dates the Father has set by his own authority" (Acts 1:7).

However, the motivation these Christians demonstrated to share their material possessions so liberally was not merely based on their "expectancy" that Christ would soon return, but also upon what they knew of Jesus' teachings during the three and a half years prior to His crucifixion, resurrection, and ascension. They took Christ's teaching seriously, probably more so than any other group of Christians at any moment in history. They responded immediately to the knowledge they had received. So should we.

3. Obeying and Believing God

The knowledge Christians had from God's unfolding revelation in New Testament days was quite different from what we have in our twentieth-century setting. Most of us have at our disposal the complete written revelation of God as it is recorded in both the Old and New Testaments. That fact is what enables us to understand God's will regarding our material possessions in a much more comprehensive way than New Testament believers. In this sense, we are more accountable both to know God's will and then to live up to the light we have.

On the other hand, the principle of obedience and faith is just as applicable to us as it was to first-century Christians. As we obey God, He honors our obedience and increases our faith. Furthermore, *He clarifies and helps us understand more fully His specific plans, enabling us to more and more respond to His will* (SCP 19).

In the book of Hebrews, one of the last books to be written and included in the New Testament, the author encourages Christians to obey God and walk by faith. After giving numerous Old Testament illustrations (Hebrews 11:1-40), he concluded, "Therefore, since we are surrounded by such a great cloud of witnesses, let us throw off everything that hinders and the sins that so easily entangle us, and let us run with perseverance the race marked out for us" (Hebrews 12:1).

No sin entangles a Christian in the affairs of this life more quickly and subtly than materialism. Though temptations to be sexually immoral are a strong force in many people's lives, the lines between right and wrong are clear-cut. To be guilty of adultery and fornication are rather nondebatable issues among Christians who believe in the values recorded In Scripture.

But where are the clear-cut lines when it comes to materialistic behaviors? Perhaps no sin is rationalized away more quickly by twentieth-century Christians than materialistic attitudes and greed. Hopefully, the principles in this book will help all of us determine where the lines between right and wrong are drawn so that we can truly obey God and learn to walk by faith in this area. As we do, God—as He always has—will honor our obedience, increase our faith, and meet our needs.

4. Applying the Teachings of Jesus Christ

Some believe that what Jesus Christ taught, particularly in the Sermon on the Mount, is not applicable to the age of the church. They feel that it applies to the messianic kingdom, when Jesus will reign and rule on earth. But, as we have seen in this book, the principles that emerge from Jesus' teachings are supracultural and verified throughout the rest of the New Testament.

This is not to say that Jesus was not speaking about a future, earthly kingdom for the nation Israel. God *will* fulfill His promises to Israel, which were first stated in the Abrahamic covenant and reaffirmed in the Davidic covenant. At that time, what Jesus taught will be particularly relevant. But the principles He shared with His disciples were practiced by the New Testament church, as well as by the church in the second and third centuries. Therefore, they should be practiced by believers in the twentieth century. Stated in terms of a principle, *all Christians today should apply the truths taught by Jesus Christ. They are normative and supracultural* (SCP 35).

5. Developing a Specific Pattern for Giving

Taking Christ's teachings seriously for today leads naturally to another important principle, particularly in terms of application. *Christians should apply the principles throughout the whole of Scripture, utilizing creative forms, patterns, and methods in their own cultures* (SCP 41). God gives us absolutes that are based upon normative "functions" and "teachings" in the Word of God. However, He does not "lock us in" to particular forms, patterns, and methods. These are nonabsolutes and culturally related.

This is the genius of Christianity, not only in terms of how the church is structured but in terms of the way Christians use their material possessions to further God's work. In some instances, Christians may donate actual produce and meat (as the children of God did in the Old Testament) to care for their spiritual leaders or to meet the needs of others in the church. In other cultures, they may convert these possessions into money, as farmers do in America. Most American Christians, however, simply give a percentage of their salaries.

God allows even more creativity for those who may be poor. Though Christians must never forget the poor widow who put all the money she had in the temple treasury, the Word of God certainly honors Christians who give their time and skills to further God's kingdom in lieu of actual material possessions. Though this approach can easily become a rationalization for Christians who want to keep more of their money for themselves, it is a freedom that God allows for those who are incapable of giving much in the way of money or possessions. This was true of the apostles who had already left everything to be involved in the work of Christ and were operating without a regular income. Though Peter and John had no silver and gold when they met the beggar in the temple, they gave what they had (Acts 3:6).

6. Putting God First in Our Financial Planning

All our economic and financial planning should be done with an intense desire to be in the will of God in every respect (SCP 58):

Now listen, you who say, "Today or tomorrow we will go to this or that city, spend a year there, *carry on business and make money.*" Why, you do not even know what will happen tomorrow. What is your life? You are a mist that appears for a little while and then vanishes. Instead, you ought to say, "If it is the Lord's will, we will live and do this or that." (James 4:13-15)

The Holy Spirit is not teaching us that it is a violation of God's will to plan ahead (see Proverbs 6:6-8; 10:5; 13:22*a*; 21:5; 24:27; 27:23; 28:19). If He were, He would be contradicting Himself. Furthermore, it is not inappropriate to "go to this city or that city" and conduct business—and even to spend "a year there," if necessary, to complete the transaction. And we would certainly be misinterpreting Scripture if we concluded that it is wrong to "make money."

James meant to convey three principles of conduct. First, we must put God at the forefront in all of our planning. That is what Jesus meant when He said that we are to "seek first his kingdom and his righteousness" (Matthew 6:33). Second, we must live our lives on earth realizing that all we are and have comes from Him. We have no right to take credit for our own accomplishments. The more God blesses, the more we should praise and thank Him. Third, when our accomplishments involve wealth, we should not focus on building a temporal kingdom for ourselves, but rather we should give generously to build the kingdom of God.

7. Excelling in Our Giving

"But just as you excel in everything—in faith, in speech, in knowledge, in complete earnestness in your love for us—*see that you also excel in this grace of giving*" (2 Corinthians 8:7). When the Corinthians were converted to Christ, they were given an abundance of spiritual gifts, or "grace gifts" (1 Corinthians 1:5, 7). Paul returned to this subject in his second letter and reminded these believers that they did excel in the gifts of the Spirit (2 Corinthians 8:7*a*). However, as Paul enumerated the ways this grace was manifested—"in faith, in speech, in knowledge"—he broadened the concept beyond spiritual gifts. He referred to "complete earnestness" and "love" (1 Corinthians 8:7)—qualities that are much more comprehensive than "spiritual gifts" and which reflect spiritual maturity—something the Corinthians lacked (1 Corinthians 3:1-3).

Consequently, when Paul encouraged the Corinthians to "also excel in this grace of giving," he was referring to more than a special spiritual gift. Just as the Corinthians were to utilize their gifts in the context of a growing manifestation of love and maturity, so they were all (not just some of them) to continue being involved in sharing their material possessions.

Paul was not simply referring to the "spiritual gift of giving" bestowed on certain individuals in the Corinthian church (see also Romans 12:6-8). He was dealing with a *spiritual quality* that all believers should and must develop if they are going to be in the will of God.

Paul was once again reminding the Corinthians that they had not responded as he had hoped. If they were as "spiritual" as they seemed to think they were (which, of course, they were not), then they should take a careful look at themselves.

In applying the principle that all Christians should excel in the grace of giving, we must recognize that some believers have a greater desire to give than others. Is this a special gift given by the Holy Spirit? It may be, but my own personal opinion is that in most instances this is simply reflective of Christians who have learned the joy of giving. They have matured in this area of their lives. They have been obedient, and they are now experiencing the blessings that come from being unselfish and benevolent.

Whatever their position on spiritual gifts, Christians should never rationalize away their responsibility to give just because they do not have a *desire* to do so and then conclude that God has not "gifted" them in this area of their lives. *It is the will of God that all of us excel in sharing our material possessions, just as it is God's will that all of us first give ourselves to the Lord* (Romans 12:1-2; SCP 72). This means that giving regularly, systematically, and proportionately is the will of God for every Christian. This is the message Paul was sending to the Corinthians. Though different Christians in Corinth would give different amounts, everyone was to be involved. And to be in the will of God, each of us must also be involved in the same way in our own local churches.

8. Responding to Government Responsibilities

When writing to the Roman Christians, Paul outlined two basic areas of obligation to the government. The first is *financial* and the second *attitudinal*: "Give everyone what you owe him; if you owe taxes, pay taxes; if revenue, then revenue; if respect, then respect; if honor, then honor" (Romans 13:7).

Here Paul clearly outlined a biblical principle that applies to every Christian in every culture of the world. *Christians should always be responsible and honest citizens in their own societies by paying all governmental taxes and revenues* (SCP 89). True, a Christian's most important position exists in relationship to Christ's body, His church (Ephesians 2:19-25). And from an eternal perspective, our true citizenship is in heaven (Ephesians 2:6). However, the Word of God teaches us that we are also citizens of our earthly society. Consequently, we have a responsibility to help maintain law and order by providing money to support people in leadership and various governmental programs (Romans 13:1-5).

Though there are certainly exceptions, the greatest problem among Christians in today's society is not an inaccurate theology regarding our responsibility to pay taxes. Rather, our challenge is to be totally honest. There are many ways to cheat the government without being detected. Unfortunately, some Christians fall prey to this kind of behavior, which is a direct violation of the will of God. Rather than taking advantage of the government, we are to pray "for kings and all those in authority, that we may live peaceful and quiet lives in all *godliness* and *holiness*" (1 Timothy 2:2).

The Word of God allows no room for rationalization in this matter. Either we are honest or dishonest. Furthermore, our honesty should not be dependent upon the ethics of our government leaders. Any form of dishonesty on their part does not make it right for Christians to engage in the same kind of sinful behavior.

9. Refocusing Our Priorities

We have noted in an earlier chapter that *God seemingly allows periodic persecutions to help Christians put more emphasis on the spiritual and eternal dimensions of life rather than on material and temporal dimensions* (SCP 42, 120). This is clear in Peter's first epistle: "These [trials] have come so that your faith—of greater worth than gold, which perishes even though refined by fire—may be proved *genuine* and may result in praise, glory and honor when Jesus Christ is revealed" (1 Peter 1:7).

Though it is the will of God generally that Christians not suffer on this earth and that we be able to "live peaceful and quiet lives in all godliness and holiness," history demonstrates that Christians need periodic awakenings to refocus their values from the "things of this world" to the "things of heaven." When life is persistently free from difficulties, and when we are able to accumulate more and more of this world's goods, we tend toward a materialistic mind-set, just as our pagan counterparts. Like them, we begin to exchange "the truth of God for a lie" and begin to worship and serve "created things rather than the Creator" (Romans 1:25). When we do, we are conforming to the pattern of this world (Romans 12:1).

What does this principle say to those of us who are living in America? Is it possible for Christians to refocus priorities before God allows external pressure to cause it to happen? I believe it is, providing we listen to and obey the Word of God and if we will learn lessons from history. As American Christians, will we refocus *now*—when it is relatively easy—or *later* when it may be a painful experience?

What about you? Are you willing to conform your life to the principles of the Word of God as they are outlined in this book? If you do, perhaps God will not allow you to face circumstances that will cause you to make these adjustments in the midst of some difficult circumstances.

10. Maintaining Proper Balance Materially and Spiritually

Christians must be on guard against establishing false distinctions between what is "material" and what is "spiritual" (SCP 123). The apostle John spoke to this issue in his first epistle because the church faced a new problem. With a great number of Gentiles believing in Christ, Christians were faced with an heretical doctrine called gnosticism. Gnostics taught that "spirit is good" but "matter is evil." Consequently, this affected their view of Jesus Christ—how He, who was very God, could inhabit a material body. John wrote to clarify the fact that Jesus Christ was in every sense the God-man, and anyone who denied that Jesus Christ had come in the flesh, could not be of God (1 John 2:22).

Regarding material possessions, John made a general statement in his first letter about the world and the things in the world. It is all-inclusive and is certainly a foundational passage for Christians to formulate their own biblical philosophy as to how they should view and use their material possessions. In many respects, it is an appropriate passage with which to end this study.

> Do not love the world or anything in the world. If anyone loves the world, the love of the Father is not in him. For everything in the world—the cravings of sinful man, the lust of his eyes and the boasting of what he has and does—comes not from the Father but from the world. (1 John 2:15-16)

The things of this world are normally not evil in themselves. What God originally created "was very good" (Genesis 1:31). However, the entrance of sin into the world's system changed everything (Romans 8:20-21). One of the results of sin has been for us to love what God has created rather than God Himself (Romans 1:25). And when we do, we are on a toboggan slide of sinful behavior, motivated by the cravings of our sinful hearts, the lusts of our eyes, and the boasting of what we have and do.

Our material possessions, of course, are an integral part of the world. And again, they are not sinful in themselves. That is why Paul made clear to Timothy that "the *love* of money is a root of all kinds of evil"—not money itself (1 Timothy 6:10).

Christians can possess material things and still use them for the glory of God. We will be tempted, however, to love what we have, so we must be on guard against the sinful cravings and lusts that are a part of our sinful nature, which has not been eradicated through conversion to Jesus Christ. That is also why Paul exhorted Timothy to "command those who are rich in this present world not to be arrogant nor to put their hope in wealth, which is so uncertain, but to put their hope in God, who richly provides us with everything for our enjoyment" (1 Timothy 6:17).

In conclusion, it should not surprise us that as believers we have difficulty harmonizing what belongs to us and what belongs to God. It is easy to say that everything we have is the Lord's (it eases our consciences) and then proceed to keep most of it for ourselves. Christians seem to fall into three negative categories when it comes to their material possessions.

THE GRACE GIVERS

First, there are the "grace givers." These people put a strong emphasis on the grace of God. Many of these people resist, even resent, any kind of approach to giving that suggests percentages and particular amounts. However, many times, when what these people actually give is recorded, measured, and evaluated, it does not come close to any form of regular or proportional giving. Unfortunately, some of these people actually use "grace" as an excuse for "license" and to cover up their love for money.

THE DEFENSIVE GIVERS

Then there are the "defensive givers." This false distinction is also manifested in the way some people react to messages on money. As long as their spiritual leaders concentrate on moral issues, they affirm what is being taught. But the moment they are exposed to what the Bible says about material possessions, they become defensive, uncomfortable, and sometimes critical. It should not surprise us that many of these people are the ones who have set up this false dichotomy in their spiritual lives and also represent those who are not regular and systematic givers. They have not integrated material possessions into their definition of spirituality.

THE SECRET GIVERS

Finally, there are the "secret givers." Another manifestation of this false dichotomy is the way in which Christians react against any form of openness regarding how they use their material possessions. They insist that this part of their lives must be totally private and secret. Unfortunately, many people (not all) who take this approach are manifesting a guilty conscience, coming up with scriptural reasons to cover up their lack of faithfulness. A true perspective and interpretation as to what Scripture teaches regarding material possessions leads to openness rather than privacy.

CONTRAST: THE BIBLICAL GIVERS

How do we recognize true "biblical givers"? They are the people who are giving regularly, systematically, and proportionately. They usually do not become defensive regarding the subject of money. In fact, they are just as excited about what the Bible teaches in this area as they are about the other great truths of Scripture. On the one hand, they enjoy the "things of this world" that have been given to them for their benefit and enjoyment. On the other hand, they do not love these things more than they love God. They do not allow their sinful cravings and the lusts of their eyes to lead them to be materialists. Neither do they allow their tendency toward pride to lead to arrogance. They have properly integrated the *material* with the *spiritual.* They are seeking first the kingdom of God (Matthew 6:33). Does this characterize your life in this world?

LET'S CHECK OURSELVES

On a scale of one to ten, circle the number that best represents how well you believe the people in your church or group practice the biblical principle found in each question.

1. Do the people in our church realize that the way they use their material possessions is important in determining the extent to which they are living in the will of God?

   VERY LITTLE   SOMEWHAT   EXTENSIVELY
   1   2   3   4   5   6   7   8   9   10

2. Are the people in our church responding according to what they already know about God's will in giving?

   VERY LITTLE   SOMEWHAT   EXTENSIVELY
   1   2   3   4   5   6   7   8   9   10

3. Are the people in our church willing to trust God in their giving, realizing that He will give them more and more clarification as to how He wants them to use their material possessions?

   VERY LITTLE   SOMEWHAT   EXTENSIVELY
   1   2   3   4   5   6   7   8   9   10

4. Do the people in our church understand and obey Jesus' teachings about material possessions?

   VERY LITTLE   SOMEWHAT   EXTENSIVELY
   1   2   3   4   5   6   7   8   9   10

5. Has our church developed programs and patterns of giving based upon a biblical theology of material possessions?

   VERY LITTLE   SOMEWHAT   EXTENSIVELY
   1   2   3   4   5   6   7   8   9   10

6. Do the people in our church do all of their economic and financial planning with an intense desire to be in the will of God?

VERY LITTLE   SOMEWHAT   EXTENSIVELY
1   2   3   4   5   6   7   8   9   10

7. Do the believers in our church excel in their financial commitment to God's work?

VERY LITTLE   SOMEWHAT   EXTENSIVELY
1   2   3   4   5   6   7   8   9   10

8. Are the people in our church faithful and honest in paying taxes and revenues to local, state, and federal governmental agencies?

VERY LITTLE   SOMEWHAT   EXTENSIVELY
1   2   3   4   5   6   7   8   9   10

9. Do Christians in our church realize that God at times allows difficulties to come into our lives in order to refocus our hearts on eternal values?

VERY LITTLE   SOMEWHAT   EXTENSIVELY
1   2   3   4   5   6   7   8   9   10

10. Have the Christians in our church learned to appreciate the things that God has created for enjoyment and, at the same time, not to love those things in a lustful or prideful way?

VERY LITTLE   SOMEWHAT   EXTENSIVELY
1   2   3   4   5   6   7   8   9   10

How to Use This Evaluation Exercise

1. Duplicate these ten questions on a separate sheet, and have each person in your group anonymously evaluate your church.
2. Tabulate the responses to find an average score. To do so, total the numbers circled in each question. Divide this total number by the number of people responding to that particular question. This will give you a "mean," or average, score.
3. Discover the greatest needs in your church by arranging the scores numerically from the highest to the lowest. Those scores that are lowest represent the areas that need immediate attention.
4. In discussing these scores and the principles involved, spend time first of all reviewing the areas of strength in your church. Spend time in prayer, thanking God for those strengths.

5. Finally, spend time discussing ways to practice the principles that are the most neglected in your church. The following questions will help:
   a. What are the areas of greatest need?
   b. What can we do that we are not doing to practice these biblical principles?
   c. What specific goals can we set up to practice these principles?
   d. What can we do *immediately*?

PERSONALIZE THIS PROJECT

Follow the procedure described at the end of chapter 1.

Appendix

The 126 Supracultural Principles of Material Possessions

This supplement is designed to help you observe supracultural principles as they emerge *chronologically* and *contextually* from God's unfolding revelation in the New Testament and as they appear in the companion volume to this book, *A Biblical Theology of Material Possessions* (Chicago: Moody, 1990). By following the sequence of principles in this appendix you will be able to see them flow from the activities and functions of the church of Jesus Christ, beginning with its founding in Jerusalem and continuing with its expansion into the New Testament world (see chart on p. 11).

The page number listed with each principle refers to its discussion in *Real Prosperity*. The accompanying symbol, which illustrates the supracultural principle, may be helpful in aiding your own understanding as well as in communicating these truths to others in a sermon or seminar setting. As you use these symbols either chronologically or thematically, the following explanations will prove helpful:

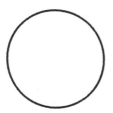

A large circle usually represents the local church. A smaller circle represents God or the glory of God.

An X usually refers to Jesus Christ.

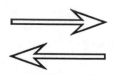

A square normally represents the world's system.

Arrows are meant to represent action, interaction, or function.

Letters usually stand for words, such as biblical characters (e.g., P = Peter; J = John).

When these three figures are seen together, they represent spiritual leaders.

THE CHURCH IN JERUSALEM

1. As Christians use their material possessions in harmony with the will of God, it
will encourage people to believe in Jesus Christ (Acts 2:47). Pp. 14-15

2. As Christians use their material possessions to meet one another's needs, it will
create love and unity in the Body of
Christ (Acts 4:32). P. 36

3. Spiritual leaders should model the way
all Christians ought to use their material
possessions (Acts 2:42). P. 44

4. Christians should be willing to make
special sacrifices in order to meet special material needs within the Body of
Christ (Acts 4:34-35). P. 53

5. A primary motivating factor for consistent Christian giving should be to meet others' needs—particularly within the Body of Christ (Acts 4:34-35). Pp. 53-54

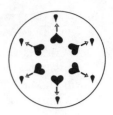

6. It is the will of God that Christians share their material possessions in order to encourage others in the Body of Christ (Acts 4:36). P. 49

7. Christians who are faithful in sharing their material possessions should be shown special appreciation (Acts 4:36). P. 38

8. Christians need to be able to observe other believers who are faithful in sharing their material possessions (Acts 4:36-37). P. 44

9. What Christians give should always be given to honor God and not themselves (Acts 4:34-36; 5:1-10). P. 68

10. God detests dishonesty, lack of integrity, and hypocrisy when it comes to giving (Acts 5:1-10). P. 68

11. Though God wants all of His children to be generous, what Christians give should always be voluntary and from a heart of love and concern (Acts 5:4). P. 71

12. It is God's will that every church have an efficient system for helping to meet the true material needs of others in the Body of Christ (Acts 6:1-7). Pp. 57-58

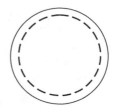

13. Spiritual leaders in the church must at times delegate the administrative responsibilities to other qualified people who can assist them in meeting material needs (Acts 6:2-4). P. 58

14. Meeting the "spiritual needs" of people and meeting the "material needs" of people require the same high standard in terms of selecting leaders to meet these needs (Acts 6:3). P. 59

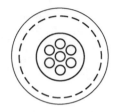

15. The way Christians use their material possessions is an important criterion for determining whether or not they are living in the will of God (Acts 2–6). P. 144

16. It is by divine design that local churches provide the primary context in which Christians are to use their material possessions to further the work of God's kingdom (Acts 2–6). Pp. 75, 124

17. Christians should respond immediately
to whatever portion of God's truth they
have received (Acts 2–6). P. 144

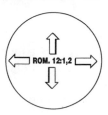

18. The expectancy of the second coming of
Jesus Christ should always be a strong
motivational factor in the way Christians
view and use their material possessions
(Acts 2–6). P. 67

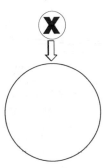

19. As we obey God, He will clarify and help
us understand His specific plans, enabling us to more and more live by faith
and respond to His will (Acts 2–6). P. 145

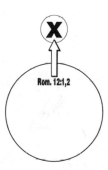

20. God's plan for Israel in the Old Testament serves as a foundational model regarding the way Christians should view
and use their material possessions today
(Acts 2–6). P. 45

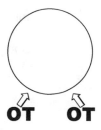

THE TEACHINGS OF JESUS CHRIST

21. Having a lot of material things often makes it difficult for people to recognize and acknowledge their need of God in salvation (Matthew 5:3). P. 25

22. Material gifts are acceptable and "well pleasing" to God only when Christians have done their part to be in harmony with their brothers and sisters in Christ (Matthew 5:24b). P. 36

23. Christians should not only give to those who love them and care for them but even to those who may resent them and even try to harm them (Matthew 5:42). P. 15

24. Christians should periodically check their motives to see if they are giving to glorify God or to glorify themselves (Matthew 6:3-4). P. 69

25. Christ wants Christians to pray for daily sustenance (Matthew 6:11). P. 85

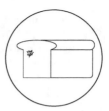

26. Whatever excess material possessions God enables Christians to accumulate should be used in creative ways to further the kingdom of God (Matthew 6:19-20). P. 99

27. Christians can determine their true perspective toward material possessions by evaluating the consistent thoughts and attitudes of their hearts (Matthew 6:21). P. 70

28. It is possible for a Christian to be in bondage to material possessions (Matthew 6:24). P. 95

29. If Christians put God first in all things, He has promised to meet their material needs (Matthew 6:33). P. 85

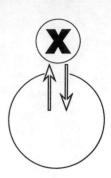

30. It is not the will of God that Christians be absorbed with worry about the future and how their material needs will be met (Matthew 6:34*a*). P. 100

31. God honors Christians in a special way when they meet the material needs of those who truly serve God (Matthew 10:42). P. 106

32. Christian children who are able should make sure that they care for their parents' physical needs (Matthew 15:4-6). P. 55

33. God will reward Christians in His eternal kingdom on the basis of the degree of sacrifice involved in their giving (Matthew 19:30). P. 91

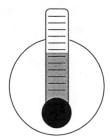

34. Christians who give regularly and faithfully are invalidating the acceptability of their gifts to God when they neglect to love God and one another (Matthew 23:23b). P. 37

35. The truths that Jesus taught about material possessions are normative and supracultural (the gospels). P. 146

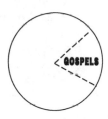

36. Christians must be careful not to evaluate subjectively what they believe is the Holy Spirit's leading when it comes to giving (John 14:25-26). P. 127

37. Christian leaders should develop an awareness of the economic structures and practices within every culture they are communicating God's truth in order to utilize these economic experiences to teach spiritual truths (Jesus' parables). P. 26

38. Spiritual leaders are responsible to teach believers in the church what God says about material possessions (the apostles' example and personal experience). P. 77

39. Economic policies for meeting the physical needs of Christian leaders who devote their full time to ministry must be built upon the totality of God's Word (Mark 6:8-13; Luke 9:1-6). P. 108

40. Believers should be motivated to share their material possessions in hopes of receiving present blessings; however, they must realize that the most important perspective in Scripture involves eternal blessings (Matthew 19:28-29). P. 89

41. Christians today should apply the principles as taught by Christ and modeled by
New Testament Christians, utilizing
forms and methods that are relevant in
their own particular cultures. P. 146

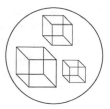

MOVING BEYOND JERUSALEM

42. God sometimes allows difficulties and discomforts to come into Christians' experiences in order to refocus their priorities on
eternal values (Acts 8:1-3). Pp. 100, 149

43. Wherever Christianity is active, some
people will attempt to use the Christian
message to benefit themselves (Acts 8:9-
25). P. 96

44. God is sometimes more patient with uninformed people who are materialistic
than He is with people who have more
direct exposure to the truth (Acts 8:9-
25). P. 28

45. Though it is often difficult for wealthy people to respond to the gospel, it is God's will that we reach them, for they can influence great segments of humanity with both their social position and their material resources (Acts 8:26-40). P. 29

46. It is God's will that Christians who have been blessed with material resources use their homes in special ways to offer hospitality to other believers (Acts 10:1-48). P. 60

47. God desires to use people with material resources who can give great segments of their time to the ministry while still providing for their families (Acts 8:5, 26, 40). P. 124

48. God desires to use Christians who may not have an abundance of material possessions but who unselfishly use what they have, including their skills, to do the work of God (Acts 9:32-43). P. 123

49. Christians who are unselfish and benevolent become a unique verification to
non-Christians that Jesus Christ is indeed
the Son of God (Acts 9:32-43). P. 16

50. God's heart responds to non-Christians
who are sincerely seeking to please Him
and who express their sincerity through
being generous with their material possessions (Acts 10:1-48). P. 29

51. When Christians in a particular culture
are excluded from social benefits because of their faith in Christ, other believers should set up some type of
welfare system to take care of valid human needs (Acts 11:19-30). P. 59

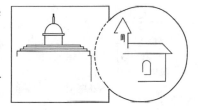

52. All Christians, according to their ability,
should be involved in sharing their material possessions to carry on God's work
in the world (Acts 11:19-30). P. 118

THE GENTILE CHURCH AND ITS EXPANDED MISSION

53. Christians in the church who do not
    have a lot of material possessions
    should not feel inferior to those who
    have more (James 1:9). P. 39

54. Christians who have a lot of material
    possessions should demonstrate humil-
    ity, realizing that their only true treasures
    are those they have stored up in heaven
    (James 1:10). P. 39

55. People who are in physical need have a
    special place in God's heart, and Chris-
    tians who help meet these needs also
    have a special place in God's heart
    (James 1:27a). P. 55

56. Christians should never show favoritism
    toward people who have an abundance
    of material possessions; conversely,
    Christians should never be prejudiced
    against people who have few material
    possessions (James 2:1). P. 40

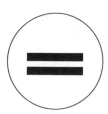

57. One of the most significant ways saving
faith is tested as to its validity and reality
is the way in which professing Christians
view and use their material possessions
(James 2:17). P. 73

58. All economic and financial planning
should be done with an intense desire to
be in the will of God in every respect
(James 4:15). P. 146

59. Non-Christians who put faith in their material possessions and who abuse and
misuse other people in order to accumulate wealth must be warned that they will
eventually be judged severely by God
Himself (James 5:1-3). P. 30

60. Accumulating wealth brings with it specific temptations for both Christians and
non-Christians (James 5:1-3). P. 96

61. Local church leaders whose primary ministry is teaching the Word of God should be given priority consideration in receiving financial support (Galatians 6:6). P. 107

62. Christians should plan ahead so they can be prepared to minister economically, first and foremost, to their fellow Christians who are in need but without neglecting non-Christians (Galatians 6:10). P. 122

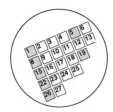

PAUL'S MISSION: THE SECOND JOURNEY

63. Christian leaders should look to fellow Christians for financial support, not to the unbelievers they are attempting to reach with the gospel (1 Thessalonians 2:9). P. 111

64. Christians should work hard to provide for their economic needs so that they are not criticized by unbelievers for being lazy and irresponsible (1 Thessalonians 4:11-12). P. 17

65. Christians should separate themselves from other Christians who are persistently irresponsible in not providing for their own economic needs (2 Thessalonians 3:6). P. 17

66. Christians who can, but do not, work for a living should not be given economic assistance (2 Thessalonians 3:10*b*). P. 60

67. Even though God has commanded that spiritual leaders be cared for financially by those they minister to, there are times when it is the part of wisdom for spiritual leaders to give up that right (1 Corinthians 9:14-15*a*). P. 111

68. Christians should set aside a certain percentage of their income on just as regular a basis as they are paid in order to be able to systematically give to God's work (1 Corinthians 16:2). P. 118

69. Those who handle and distribute monies that are given to God's work should be above reproach in all respects and should be held accountable (1 Corinthians 16:3-4). P. 77

70. Every local body of believers needs real-life examples of other churches that are positive models in the area of giving (2 Corinthians 8:1-2). P. 46

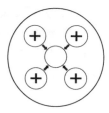

71. Christians need to be held accountable when they make financial commitments to God's work (2 Corinthians 8:6, 10-11; 9:3). P. 123

72. It is God's will that all Christians excel in the grace of giving (2 Corinthians 8:7). P. 148

73. God does not want Christians to respond to a command to share their material possessions but, rather, to respond out of hearts of love that reflect sincere appreciation for His gift of salvation (2 Corinthians 8:8-9). P. 72

74. God honors believers' gifts once they begin to give regularly and systematically, even though they may not be able to give as proportionately as they will be able to once they have their economic lives in order (2 Corinthians 8:10-12). P. 120

75. It is not the will of God that some Christians cannot meet their physical needs while other Christians with abundance could help them in their time of need (2 Corinthians 8:13-14). P. 56

76. It is the will of God that no one particular Christian leader should have to handle the financial needs of the Christian community alone (2 Corinthians 8:16-19, 22-24; 9:3-4). P. 78

77. Christians who are generous will motivate other Christians to also be generous (2 Corinthians 9:2). P. 49

78. Christians who make commitments financially should be on guard against embarrassing their spiritual leaders, as well as themselves, by being negligent in following through on their commitments (2 Corinthians 9:3-4). P. 122

79. God wants Christians to take a step of faith and trust Him to enable them to be able to give certain amounts of money based upon future earnings (2 Corinthians 9:5*a*). P. 120

80. Christians should organize and plan their giving in a systematic way so that they can give generously and not respond in a grudging fashion (2 Corinthians 9:5*b*). P. 121

81. Christians who are generous in their giving will receive generous blessings; conversely, Christians who are not generous in their giving will not receive generous blessings (2 Corinthians 9:6). P. 87

82. Every Christian is ultimately responsible to give to God on the basis of his own heart decision (2 Corinthians 9:7). P. 71

83. When Christians are faithful in their giving, God has promised to meet their needs (2 Corinthians 9:8). P. 86

84. When Christians are generous, God has promised to enable them to continue to be generous (2 Corinthians 9:11). P. 87

85. Generous Christians cause others to praise and worship God (2 Corinthians 9:11-13). P. 50

86. People respect and love Christians who are unselfish and generous (2 Corinthians 9:14). P. 37

87. The local church is God's primary context for maintaining accountability in the area of material possessions. Pp. 75, 124

88. It is important that Christian leaders maintain a high level of communication in order to enable Christians to be obedient to God's will in the way they use their material possessions. P. 79

PAUL'S MISSION: THE THIRD JOURNEY AND IMPRISONMENT

89. Christians should always be responsible and honest citizens in their own societies by paying all governmental taxes and revenues (Romans 13:6-7). P. 148

90. Christians who owe people money or goods should always pay what they owe (Romans 13:8). P. 132

91. All Christians have an obligation to support God's work in material ways (Romans 15:27). P. 126

92. Christians must never take economic advantage of poor people, whether Christians or non-Christians (Exodus 22:25). P. 134, 136

93. Christians who obey God's Word will be able not only to meet their own economic needs but also to help others who are in need (Psalm 37:21). P. 134

94. Christians must set the example of being gracious to people who have borrowed money with good intentions and then have faced crises beyond their control that have made it hard for them to repay on time (Deuteronomy 15:1-3). P. 136

95. Before Christians borrow money for any purpose, they should consider all of the circumstances and seek wisdom from others who can help them evaluate all aspects of the decision, including the risks involved (Proverbs 22:7). P. 137

96. Christians who guarantee another person's loan should make sure they are able to repay the loan while meeting other financial obligations, including their indebtedness to the Lord (Proverbs 22:26-27). P. 138

97. Christians are out of God's will when they knowingly borrow money that they cannot pay back according to a predetermined agreement (Romans 13:8). P. 139

98. Christians are out of God's will when they cannot give God the "firstfruits" of their income because they have obligated themselves to pay off debts (1 Corinthians 16:2). P. 139

99. Christians who put God first in their lives may open the door for people to take material advantage of them (Philemon 18). P. 31

100. Christian leaders should utilize methods of communication that create both a sense of obligation and a spirit of spontaneity and freedom (Philemon 14, 18-19). P. 80

101. Christian leaders should not hesitate to ask for help when there is a need, both for others and for themselves (Philemon 20-22). P. 112

102. Christians may face criticism or even retaliation when their commitment to do God's will conflicts with others' materialistic value systems (Acts 19:23-41). P. 31

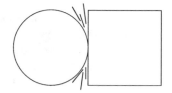

103. Christians should work hard to make an honest living, not only to take care of their own needs, but to help others in need (Ephesians 4:28). P. 57

104. Christian employees should work hard and serve their employers (both Christians and non-Christians) as if they are actually serving the Lord (Colossians 3:23-24). P. 18

105. Christian employers should always treat their employees fairly in every respect (Colossians 4:1). P. 19

106. Christians who faithfully support God's servants in material ways create unusual joy in the hearts of those who receive their gifts (Philippians 1:3-5). P. 107

107. Christians who faithfully support God's servants in material ways enrich those servants' prayer lives by making it a joyful experience (Philippians 1:3-5). P. 108

108. Christians who make special sacrifices to help meet the material needs of God's servants should be honored in special ways by others in the Body of Christ (Philippians 2:29-30). Pp. 38, 88

109. God's servants should be open and honest about their material needs, but they should avoid any form of dishonesty and manipulation by playing on others' sympathy (Philippians 4:11). P. 61

110. All Christians should learn to be content in the difficult times as well as in the prosperous times (Philippians 4:12). P. 101

111. Christian leaders who make their living in the ministry should serve Jesus Christ with the view that they are storing up treasures in heaven for those who support them financially (Philippians 4:14-17). P. 112

112. God's promise to meet needs applies to the church as well as to individual believers in that church (Philippians 4:19). P. 89

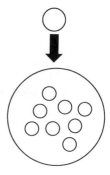

THE FINAL YEARS OF THE NEW TESTAMENT ERA

113. All spiritual leaders in the church should be generous Christians who are willing to use their material possessions to serve those they shepherd and lead (1 Timothy 3:2; Titus 1:6, 8). P. 44

114. Christians who occupy leadership roles in the church should be totally trustworthy when it comes to financial matters (1 Timothy 3:2-3, 8; Titus 1:7-8). P. 76

115. The selection of people who receive consistent help from the church should be based upon specific scriptural guidelines (1 Timothy 5:3-16). P. 58

116. Pastors and teachers who are hardworking, efficient, and productive in the ministry should be rewarded financially (1 Timothy 5:17). P. 107

117. A Christian's first priority should be to focus on godliness and contentment rather than on riches, which often bring discontentment (1 Timothy 6:6-10, 17-19). P. 101

118. So-called Christian leaders who are teaching false doctrine and manipulating people in order to pursue dishonest gain should be silenced (Titus 1:10-11). P. 81

119. As the Day of Christ draws nearer, Christians should avoid the increasing tendency to intensify love for self, money, and pleasure (2 Timothy 3:1-2*a*, 4*b*-5). P. 97

120. God allows periodic persecution to help Christians to put more emphasis on the spiritual and eternal dimensions of life rather than on the material and temporal (1 Peter 1:7, 18-19, 23-25*a*; 2:5, 11-12; 4:9; 5:2). Pp. 100, 149

121. All Christians are to show hospitality, not only to those believers in a specific local Christian community but to those whom they may not know personally (Hebrews 13:2, 5, 16). P. 63

122. Christians should be on guard against false teachers who are motivated by selfishness and greed and who exploit people with fabricated stories (2 Peter 2:3*a*, 14*b*; Jude 12*a*). P. 109

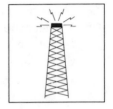

123. Christians must be on guard against establishing false distinctions between what is "material" and what is "spiritual" (1 John 2:15-16). P. 150

124. Christians should not support religious teachers and leaders who claim to be Christians but who deny that Jesus Christ came as God in the flesh (2 John 10-11). P. 110

125. Christian leaders who receive their financial support from the church they serve must be on guard against a selfish refusal to share financial help with other Christian leaders who are in need (3 John 5, 8). P. 113

126. Christians must be on guard against self-deception and rationalization when they are living in an affluent society (Revelation 3:17-18). P. 98

Moody Press, a ministry of the Moody Bible Institute,
is designed for education, evangelization, and edification.
If we may assist you in knowing more about Christ
and the Christian life, please write us without obligation:
Moody Press, c/o MLM, Chicago, Illinois 60610.